Exchange Rates and Merchandise Trade in Liberalised India

This book examines the linkages between exchange rates and India's merchandise trade since the 1990s. It looks at India's trade in the post-liberalisation period through its two main components, commodities and trading partners, and provides a bird's eye view through aggregate analyses accompanied by a historical narrative of the evolution of trade and exchange rate dynamics. Presenting a comprehensive analysis of bilateral and product-specific trade, the book explores the impact of exchange rate on labour intensive sectors and charts out major development. It also offers compelling evidence to suggest that if some commodities are identified as integral to India's export plans, then the impact of exchange rate must be weighed by the Reserve Bank of India (RBI) prior to a market intervention.

This timely volume will be of interest to scholars and researchers of economics, business and finance, development studies, trade, business, and industry as well as practitioners, think-tanks, and policy makers.

Suranjali Tandon is Assistant Professor at the National Institute of Public Finance and Policy, New Delhi, an autonomous institute of the Ministry of Finance, Government of India, and has been a consultant with its tax research team. She completed her PhD in Economics from Jawaharlal Nehru University, New Delhi.

T0382801

Critical Political Economy of South Asia

Series editors: C. P. Chandrasekhar and Jayati Ghosh, both at the *Centre for Economic Studies and Planning, Jawaharlal Nehru University, New Delhi, India*

At a time when countries of the South Asian region are in a state of flux, reflected in far-reaching economic, political, and social changes, this series aims to showcase critical analyses of some of the central questions relating to the direction and implications of those changes. Volumes in the series focus on economic issues and integrate these with incisive insights into historical, political and social contexts. Drawing on work by established scholars as well as younger researchers, they examine different aspects of political economy that are essential for understanding the present and have an important bearing on the future. The series will provide fresh analytical perspectives and empirical assessments that will be useful for students, researchers, policy makers, and concerned citizens.

The first books in the series cover themes such as the economic impact of new regimes of intellectual property rights, the trajectory of financial development in India, changing patterns of consumption expenditure and trends in poverty, health, and human development in India, and land relations. Future volumes will deal with varying facets of economic processes and their consequences for the countries of South Asia.

Global Players and the Indian Car Industry
Trade, Technology and Structural Change
Jatinder Singh

Industrial Policy Challenges for India
Global Value Chains and Free Trade Agreements
Smitha Francis

Exchange Rates and Merchandise Trade in Liberalised India
Suranjali Tandon

For more information about this series, please visit: www.routledge.com/Critical-Political-Economy-of-South-Asia/book-series/CRPE

Exchange Rates and Merchandise Trade in Liberalised India

Suranjali Tandon

Routledge
Taylor & Francis Group

LONDON AND NEW YORK

First published 2020 by Routledge

2 Park Square, Milton Park, Abingdon, Oxon, OX14 4RN
605 Third Avenue, New York, NY 10017

Routledge is an imprint of the Taylor & Francis Group, an informa business

First issued in paperback 2020

British Library Cataloguing-in-Publication Data
A catalogue record for this book is available from the British Library

Library of Congress Cataloging-in-Publication Data
A catalog record for this book has been requested

ISBN: 978-1-138-58520-1 (hbk)
ISBN: 978-0-367-72792-5 (pbk)

Typeset in Sabon
by Apex CoVantage, LLC

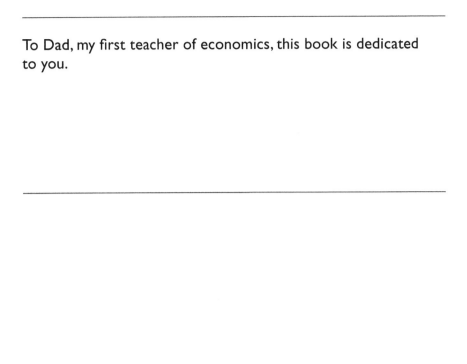

To Dad, my first teacher of economics, this book is dedicated to you.

Contents

Figures and tables

Figures

Tables

Preface and acknowledgements

The journey of a book begins with an idea. Struggling to find a contemporary issue that had not been adequately addressed, all too familiar to any PhD student, I began researching. A series of discussions with Professor Jayati Ghosh helped me fix the idea that was to occupy me for the next four years. It is always tempting to switch to something more interesting or *with the times*. But current affairs, too, had been propitious. In 2013, the rupee came under severe pressure, and the din grew louder on the subject of whether this meant any good for the exports or the external account. It was worrying that the matter had been dealt with through concise aggregate econometrics or narrow disaggregate analysis. Therefore, the precise role of exchange rate movements in influencing trade and the rationale for observed relations in India seemed underexplored. To fill this gap, I began a journey that now has shaped into this book. Piecing together evidence from disparate sets of data and analysing all these for the period post liberalisation was a slow yet rewarding process. To put together the results in a coherent form was the most challenging bit of the work. To build a narrative, I searched for months to find a common thread through all the tiny empirical stories. The work slowly began to take shape. In this book, there is compelling evidence to suggest that the discussion on this subject may be re-oriented. A new perspective to a long-debated question, I suggest that policy must not be blinded by the aggregate picture. A more structural issue of product composition of trade can have a significant bearing on the trade and exchange rate nexus.

To carry an idea to completion needs a caring critic, and for this I must thank Professor Ghosh. She carefully read and commented on many versions of the chapters. This book in its final form is the result of all her invaluable comments and inputs.

To write a book such as this requires equal proportions of academic rigour and ability to question one's work. I thank Sayantani Chakravarty for inspiring rigour and for acquiescing to impromptu discussions at unearthly hours.

I thank Dr. R Kavita Rao for questioning the obvious and compelling me to think critically.

Lastly, for an idea to be conceived, there must be a vision and the will to pursue. I thank Ranjan Tandon for being the inspiration that he is.

Chapter 1

Introduction

Episodes of sharp exchange rate depreciation reignite interest in its possible economic ramifications. During such times, the central bank, in an economy with a managed float, is confronted with the difficult choice either to intervene to stall such depreciation or to resort to inaction. The decision to intervene is based on a variety of macroeconomic considerations. However, one consideration that often gets cited to discourage the central bank from stepping in is that depreciation could make the country's exports relatively competitive as well as render imports dearer. The change in prices denominated in foreign currency would in turn correct the imbalance in the trade account. Those familiar with the empirical literature on the subject know that such assumed causation or adjustment may vary circumstantially. The lack of agreement on the direction of impact is rooted in theory, where two schools of thought – Keynesians and monetarists – offer alternate explanations of the processes of adjustment that ensue following a depreciation.

Within the Keynesian theoretical tradition, two main explanations are provided for the processes of adjustment: the elasticities approach and the absorption approach. As per the elasticities approach, depreciation of the domestic currency must result in higher export proceeds[1] and lower imports if the demand and supply elasticities permit. The condition when such an impact will be realised is formally called the Marshall-Lerner Condition.[2] This condition, put simply, requires that when currency depreciates, a country that does not hold a dominant position in the global market must have an elasticity of exports and imports that together exceed one, for the trade balance to improve. Even when the elasticities are such as to lead to a positive response of the trade balance to exchange rate depreciation, pre-contracted trade along with invoicing of trade in foreign currency may delay such a response. Such lagged improvement in the trade balance is referred to as the J-curve effect. That is, a temporary worsening of the trade deficit is followed by an improvement.

The other Keynesian approach – which is known as the absorption approach – looks at the balance of payments as a reflection of the macroeconomic aggregates in the economy. In this case, the impact of the exchange rate is to affect absorption (expenditure) differently from income: so depreciation improves the balance of trade to the extent that expenditure, which is consumption plus investment, increases less than income. Here, imports are seen as a function of the level of income.

These approaches assume that a nominal depreciation results in a real devaluation as well, even if not to the same extent. The real exchange rate is the nominal exchange rate expressed in domestic currency unit deflated by the ratio of domestic to foreign prices. Thus, for the Keynesian process of adjustment to take place, the relative prices would have to remain unchanged.

By contrast, monetarists argue that changes in the nominal exchange rate result in changes in domestic prices such that there is no change in the real exchange rate, and therefore nominal devaluation has no impact on trade. The purchasing power parity hypothesis posits a positive (45-degree line) relationship between the exchange rate and the domestic price level. This occurs because individuals demand more of the currency with the higher purchasing power, so domestic price change results in nominal depreciation. Similarly, nominal exchange rate depreciation results in an increase in domestic prices to the point that there is no change in the real exchange rate. Most monetarist theorists now accept this as a long-run tendency and accept that some short-run effects of nominal exchange rates on the trade balance may occur.

The above discussion provides the theoretical grounding. However, as is often observed, the question of whether exchange rate movements can impact the merchandise trade does not have a simple answer. In 2014, I undertook a statistical analysis of the exports and imports of 16 major trading countries – Austria, Brazil, China, Denmark, France, Germany, Italy, Japan, Malaysia, Mexico, the Philippines, Norway, the Netherlands, Singapore, Switzerland, and the United Kingdom (UK), for the period 1980–2010. The estimated results show that for countries such as China, Brazil, Malaysia, the Philippines, and Mexico, exchange rate depreciation led to an improvement in the trade balance. As for the countries in the Euro Zone, the response of the exchange rate is not symmetric across member countries. For France and Italy, an improvement is observed in trade deficit with depreciation, whereas the obverse is observed for the rest. Without further detail, the evidence provided here makes clear that there are no clear-cut responses. Work by other authors, specifically focussing on India, does not present a clear answer to this question. Motivated by these results observed in my earlier work, and by those for India – which, until I began this study, were largely restricted to the pre-liberalisation era – I chose to examine the question specifically in the context of post liberalisation.

Other than the dearth of systematic study on the subject, developments in the India economy were an even more compelling reason to pursue the theme of research. In 2013, the Indian rupee depreciated sharply. Responding to such sharp depreciation, experts and policy makers presented different views. A few suggested that the exchange rate depreciation could encourage exports. The fact that this was being conjectured, and no evidence was available to conclude, created the need to examine this in the Indian context. In trying to unravel the dynamics underlying such an observed relationship, a series of evidence was found and is presented in this book to explain why and when the exchange rate changes are expected to influence merchandise trade.

The book begins by introducing the reader to market for exchange rates. The whole process of adjustment – beginning from the source of the observed exchange rate movements, to price changes, and finally the response of the trade account – must be understood prior to interpreting the statistical results. Further, to say why we see the results we do, it is important to have a reasonable understanding of the structure of trade and the principal drivers of this trade. This book, therefore, begins by providing a broad overview of India's external account followed by the first set of econometric results to show the exchange rate–trade relationship for the overall economy. The exploration of these results opened up a new dimension for examination. It was not unknown, in the case of India, that the exchange rate could elicit different responses for trade in different commodities. However, this evidence was not systematically presented in a single document, neither was there any attempt to rationalise the impact observed for the overalls using commodity composition. Building on the preliminary findings that the exchange rate will have a certain kind of impact depending on the structure of the trade, and the underlying regulatory and market dynamics, this book provides detailed evidence for top items exported and imported by India (Chapter 3), then proceeds to analyse bilateral trade (Chapter 4).

Therefore, within the broad theme – whether exchange rate changes affect merchandise trade – the book asks if there are patterns that explain the evident impact or the lack thereof. While doing so, the various forces at play, such as government intervention, international agreements, and regulatory sanctions, are documented. The details, though seemingly a digression, in Chapters 2 and 3 are veritable to the principal question being addressed.

The analysis carried out in each chapter is for the period after liberalisation. However, I must caution the reader that these may not be consistent across chapters. This is because the data available to present a cogent argument, using price and quantity information, are taken from alternative sources. The information available across such sources of information is for different time periods presented herein. The positive outcome of this exercise is that despite the disparate time periods selected across different analyses, the results remain consistent. That is, the results remain unchanged even if the time period varies for the disaggregate analysis based on commodity and country.

Going back to the important question: should the Central Bank intervene at all, and would letting exchange rates be bring about the desired change?

The results presented here allow policy makers to reflect the different kinds of changes that are set in motion once the exchange rate appreciates or depreciates sharply. In fact, at the end of this book, we may be able to say whether the exchange rate remains a tool that the government can employ to influence exports and imports.

Notes

1 Except for the perverse cases where the demand for exports is completely inelastic.

2 $\left| \dfrac{\epsilon_x \left(\eta_x - 1 \right)}{\epsilon_x + \eta_x} + \dfrac{\eta_m \left(\epsilon_m + 1 \right)}{\epsilon_m + \eta_m} \right| > 0;$

Where ϵ_x and ϵ_m denote the elasticity of supply of exports and imports respectively, and, η_m and η_x are the elasticity of demand for exports and imports respectively.

Chapter 2

Exchange rate movements and trade patterns in India

Introduction

Occasions of sharp exchange rate depreciation tend to revive the unresolved debate on whether such depreciation can augment a country's exports. The evidence for different countries does little to resolve this debate. It is seen that movements in exchange rates have differing impacts on the trade balances of different countries (Tandon, 2014). For this precise purpose, this book presents systematic evidence for India in the period post liberalisation. The observed causalities derive their explanation from history and the structure of economic activity.

As is known, the exchange rate system in India has evolved from a fixed pegged to the pound sterling in the 1970s to the present managed float. The conduct of monetary policy varies across regimes. In the case of a fixed exchange rate, there is an explicit commitment to a peg whereas a liberalised or floating exchange rate restricts the intervention by the Central Bank, if it intervenes at all, to extra-ordinary circumstances. Theoretically, the merit of the floating exchange rate is that it allows an economy to pursue an independent monetary policy. The floating exchange rate system also redistributes the burden of adjustment from the domestic economy to the external account in the circumstance of a crisis. However, the reduced burden of adjustment on the domestic economy comes at the expense of increased volatility. India has observed several episodes of pronounced volatility and sharp current account imbalances.

The theory of purchasing power parity suggests that movements in the nominal exchange rate are accompanied by adjustments in domestic prices so as to keep the real exchange rate unchanged. However, there is evidence that suggests the contrary for various countries, including India. That is, prices do not adjust so as to restore such *equilibrium*. As a result, an exchange rate depreciation would alter the price of a good expressed in foreign currency. This in turn would result in a change in quantity demanded. This chapter works through these mechanics of price adjustments. First, it examines the co-movement in real and nominal exchange rate. This is to show if prices do adjust in response to the exchange rate or if there is any *pass through*. Further, documenting the shift in production, such as significant reliance on import for inputs, this chapter finally presents estimates that show the precise overall relationship between exchange rate and merchandise trade. The academic literature that explores this issue is largely confined to pre-liberalisation, thus necessitating that the question be asked for the period after liberalisation.

Evolution of India's exchange rate regime

India's exchange rate regime has evolved over time, from the post-independence par value system to the existing managed float. The switch in the exchange rate regime is the result of pressures from both the international economy and its own external account.

In 1947, India adopted the par value system as part of the Bretton Woods arrangement and pegged its exchange rate at one rupee equal to 4.15 grains of fine gold, within a band of +/− 1 per cent. Under the par value system, the rupee's value was fixed in terms of gold, and the intervention currency was the pound sterling. This par value was revised on two occasions, the first being the devaluation of 1949, which resulted in a par value of 1.83 fines of gold. The second occasion when India devalued its currency significantly was in 1966, when the rupee-to-US-dollar exchange rate increased from 4.76 to 7.50. This exchange rate was maintained till the collapse of the Bretton Woods system in 1971. Upon the collapse, India pegged its currency to the pound sterling. However, this arrangement lasted only for four years, and in order to overcome the weakness of a single currency peg, the Indian rupee was pegged to a basket of 14 currencies, later reduced to four. The currencies and their respective weights in the peg were kept confidential in order to avoid speculation. In 1978, as a measure to liberalise the foreign exchange market, intra-day trade in foreign exchange by domestic banks was permitted. There was an overwhelming response by banks, in response to which the "Guidelines for Internal Control over Foreign Exchange Business" were framed in 1981. At that time, the market for foreign exchange was tightly regulated and was governed by the Foreign Exchange Regulation Act. As a consequence of such regulations, an informal market for foreign exchange sprung up. During the 1980s, there were capital controls in place which restricted foreign direct investment and portfolio flows only to public sector bond issues, while disallowing foreign equity holdings in domestic companies. Even the interest paid on NRI deposits was subject to controls.

The second episode of significant devaluation was in July 1991. The devaluation was attributable to two developments in the global economy – weaker demand for exports due to slower growth of output for trading partners, and the increase in the oil prices on account of the Gulf War. These led to a widening of the current account deficit (3 per cent of GDP) and the depletion of the foreign currency assets to less than a billion dollars. In order to deal with the crisis, the RBI devalued the currency by 23 per cent in two phases on 1 and 3 July 1991. The crisis and its resolution marked the end of the pegged exchange rate regime for India. In March 1992, the Liberalized Exchange Rate Management System (LERMS) was put in place as per which a transitional dual exchange rate system – an exchange rate for select government and private transactions and a market-determined rate for others – was adopted. In this system, the RBI declared its rate and the Foreign Exchange Dealers Association of India (FEDAI) intimated their *Indicative Rate* (market rate) to the Authorised Dealers for dollars, mark, yen, and pound sterling. As a part of the LERMS, import of gold was permitted in order to thwart the thriving informal market for foreign exchange. In March 1993, the dual rates converged, and the market-determined exchange rate regime was introduced. In 1994, the current account was fully convertible and the process of capital account liberalisation was initiated. Despite the exchange rate being market-determined, the RBI has intervened from time to time to stabilise the value of the rupee. Although the RBI has intervened both during periods of excess demand and supply, it has not done so with a predetermined target or band around the exchange rate (Jalan, 2003).

The evolution of the exchange rate, i.e. INR vis-à-vis the US dollar, associated with the switch in the regime can be traced in Figure 2.1. With the liberalisation of the external account, it is seen that the exchange rate has depreciated over the years 1993–2014, with the exception of the years 2003–07 when the inflows on account of External Commercial Borrowings (ECB) and Investment recorded a phenomenal increase.[1]

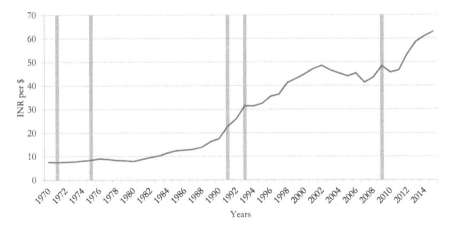

Figure 2.1 INR per $ 1970–2014

Source: Database on Indian Economy, RBI

Note: The vertical grey lines signify year of major change

With the liberalisation of the external account, the institutions and participants in the market for foreign exchange have also transformed. The market
is now comprised of spot and derivative transactions, the latter consisting
of futures, swaps, and options. According to the Triennial Central Bank
Survey of Foreign Exchange and Derivatives Market Activity conducted by
the Bank for International Settlements (BIS), daily average turnover in India
jumped almost fivefold from US$7 billion in April 2004 to US$34 billion in
April 2007; global turnover over the same period rose by only 66 per cent
from US$2.4 trillion to US$4.0 trillion (Dua and Ranjan, 2010). The rise
of trading in foreign exchange derivative markets along with the development of markets for non-deliverable forwards (NDFs) in countries such as
Singapore and Dubai are an added dimension of the present market for
foreign exchange. Goyal et al. (2013) show that the market for NDFs have
an impact on the exchange rate in *onshore markets*.

Thus, exchange rate or the value of INR, which was determined by the
RBI during the pre-liberalisation period, is now determined by a complex
network of markets.

Liberalisation of the external account has also exposed the Indian
economy to the vicissitudes of global financial capital flows. Thus, RBI
has not entirely stepped out of its shoes of exchange rate manager; it still
intervenes, though sparingly. The opening of the capital account was met
with large capital inflows, both direct and portfolio, during March 1993
to July 1995. The resulting capital account surplus led to appreciation of
the exchange rate. The expectation of an adverse impact on India's competitiveness prompted the RBI to step in to purchase dollars, thereby stall-
ing this appreciation and simultaneously building up foreign exchange
reserves that increased from $6.08 billion to $20.8 billion during the
aforementioned period. However, the optimism following this appreciation was short-lived. During the last quarter of 1995, the contagion effect
of the Mexican crisis led to renewed volatility and sharp depreciation of
the rupee, despite *benign* macroeconomic conditions (Prakash, 2014). The
RBI stepped in yet again by selling its foreign exchange reserves and impos-
ing administrative controls.[2] Foreign capital trickled in to emerging market
economies after the Mexican crisis. Lower inflows manifested in another
round of depreciation in 1996. The RBI used direct forward sales to elimi-
nate volatility. As a result, the foreign exchange reserves fell to US$15.9
billion in February 1996 from US$19 billion prior to the Mexican crisis.
During the same year, the RBI, in a move to encourage inflows, eased the
ECB norms among other reforms that it introduced,[3] resulting in relatively
more expensive trade credit.

However, the worst was yet to come. In 1997, the contagion effect of the
Asian Financial Crisis preceded by the downturn in the domestic economy
spurred another round of depreciation in August 1997. Contributing to
these factors was the overwhelming response from market participants who

had been largely unhedged or oversold to cover their positions as well as those who had taken on foreign currency debt to exploit the interest rate differential. In response, the RBI turned into a net seller of foreign exchange during November 1997. The exchange rate depreciation stalled until May 1998, when the sanctions imposed on India for Pokhran testing, sovereign rating downgrade, and the lower capital inflows to EMEs on account of the Asian Financial Crisis led to renewed depreciation. The RBI once again was compelled to intervene by introducing special incentives for exporters in addition to its sale of foreign exchange that continued till July 1998, by which time its sales had touched \$3.2 billion and its intervention in the forward exchange market had led to the accumulation of forward liabilities worth \$40 million.

On the flip side were 2003 and 2004, the two years marked by the sharp appreciation of the rupee against the dollar with a surge in capital inflows. To stem this appreciation, the Reserve Bank intervened in the market for foreign exchange by purchasing, in the net, \$30 billion of foreign exchange assets. In fact, in 2007–08, the massive appreciation (see Figure 2.1) of the rupee against the US dollar of the exchange rate because of capital inflows was met with the largest net purchase of dollars since liberalisation, of \$78.2 billion. The global financial crisis following the collapse of Lehmann Brothers in 2008, and the 2011 Eurozone debt crisis, reversed the trend of subdued volatility and exchange rate appreciation, with the subsequent years followed by depreciation of the rupee. In fact, during 2011–12, the rupee depreciated against major international currencies[4,5] (see Figure 2.2

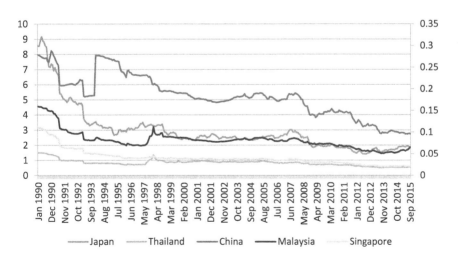

Figure 2.2 Nominal exchange rate (foreign currency per rupee)

Source: Calculated from IFS, IMF

for INR's value against Japan's yen and China's yuan). The RBI intervened in the foreign exchange market through sale of dollars during 2011–12. In May 2013, the announcement of the withdrawal of Quantitative Easing by the US Fed led to depreciation of emerging market currencies. India, with its rising current account deficit, witnessed a sharp depreciation. In less than six months, the rupee fell by 14.7 per cent, from a value of 54.38/USD (April 2013) to 63.75/USD (September 2013). The rupee touched an all-time low at 68.4 per USD in August 2013. In response, the RBI took monetary policy measures that primarily operated through the reduction of liquidity in the banking sector. Some of these measures included open market sales of government securities,[6] an increase in the MSF rate,[7] and limiting the overall funds under LAF. Other than these, the RBI made net sales of US$10.8 billion in the FOREX market during the period May to August 2013. Further, other measures were introduced; for example, 20 per cent of imported gold was to be used for exports. In the months that followed, the rupee no longer depreciated as sharply. It depreciated 1 per cent in 2014–15, and approximately 5 per cent in 2015–16; however, this depreciation was not as large as that witnessed by other developing countries such as Russia and Brazil (more than 30 per cent in 2015–16). During these two years, the RBI continued to purchase dollars to build up reserves.

This historical experience brings out an important fact about the exchange rate; i.e. despite liberalisation, the exchange rate market has been subject to sporadic intervention by the RBI to curb volatility, which arises predominantly on account of international events. Only recently has the RBI allowed the rupee to depreciate and has continued to accumulate FOREX reserves in times of appreciation.

The RBI specifically states that its objective is to curb excessive volatility of currency value. The efforts in this regard have been shown to have been successful. Studies such as Pattanaik and Sahoo (2003), Kohli (2000) demonstrate that the volatility of the exchange rate has been curtailed by the intervention undertaken by RBI.

To demonstrate that this has been the case, exchange rate volatility is calculated using different methods. One such method, i.e. first difference of the logarithmic value[8] of bilateral and effective exchange rates, is selected. The volatility for the nominal trade weighted effective exchange rate and the bilateral rate (versus the USD) is pronounced during episodes of global crisis. Interestingly, the volatility of the rupee has been relatively sharp vis-à-vis the US dollar (see Figures 2.3 and 2.4), and this has increased in the years after 2003, which includes the years when the rupee appreciated. This increase in the volatility of the exchange rate has been associated with the increase in capital inflows that are volatile in nature.

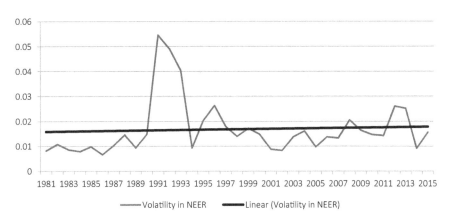

Figure 2.3 Volatility in nominal effective exchange rate

Source: Computed

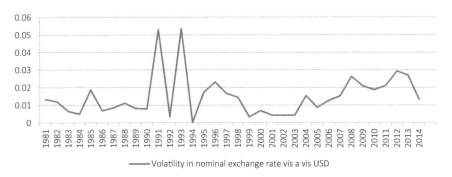

Figure 2.4 Volatility in nominal exchange rate (vis-à-vis USD)

Source: Computed, based on NEER data from Database on Indian Economy, RBI

Major components of India's balance of payments and determinants of exchange rate

The opening up of India's capital account ushered in private capital flows. These flows in fact make up a major portion of the external account. In the overall balance of payments, merchandise exports and portfolio inflows constitute two major sources of foreign exchange inflow to India; during the financial year 2014–15, the two accounted for 54 per cent of total inflows (Figure 2.5). In the case of outflows, merchandise imports account for approximately half of the foreign exchange outflows, followed by portfolio

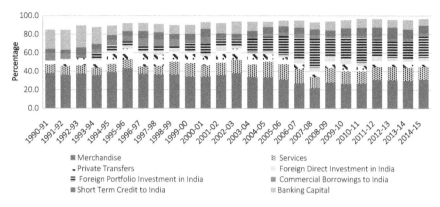

Legend:
- Merchandise
- Private Transfers
- Foreign Portfolio Investment in India
- Short Term Credit to India
- Services
- Foreign Direct Investment in India
- Commercial Borrowings to India
- Banking Capital

Figure 2.5 Composition of inflows (% share)

Source: Database on Indian Economy, RBI

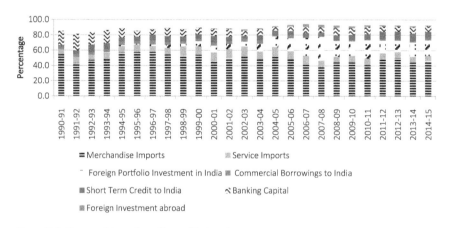

Legend:
- Merchandise Imports
- Foreign Portfolio Investment in India
- Short Term Credit to India
- Foreign Investment abroad
- Service Imports
- Commercial Borrowings to India
- Banking Capital

Figure 2.6 Composition of outflows (% share)

Source: Database on Indian Economy, RBI

outflows that consist of repatriation of foreign investment in India (Figure 2.6). In 2014–15, the outflow on account of just these two components was 66 per cent.

The other two significant components of the balance of payments are short term credit and banking capital. While short term credit comprises all lending by commercial institutions for a period of less than one year, banking capital consists of assets and liabilities of commercial banks, which includes NRI deposits and foreign currency holdings.[9]

Further, if one analyses the net balance of each of these components, it is observed that while the merchandise trade has been in deficit over the period 1996 Q1 to 2013–14 Q4, portfolio flows have fluctuated between net inflows and outflows depending on the state of the global economy; whereas remittances, trade in services, and FDI have in the net been positive (surplus) (Figure 2.7). Taking the net balance for each of these balance of payments items as a percentage of total GDP, it is observed that over the years, the trade deficit has widened, and this has been more pronounced post 2003–04, when the volume of imports increased and world crude and commodity prices rose and were accompanied by flat or declining relative unit value of exports (shown in Section 2.4). Portfolio flows, commercial borrowing, and banking capital are all major sources of capital inflows, and in the net they have been fluctuating, attributable largely to global economic conditions. Remittances and FDI have been stable as a proportion of GDP over the years, with a reversal in the trend of FDI inflows following the global financial crisis.

The external balance is largely driven by portfolio flows and merchandise trade, where the volatility in the former is expected to influence movements in foreign exchange rate. During the period of capital inflows, the exchange rate is expected to appreciate, and any reversal in such inflows would do the opposite. Evidence for India suggests that higher capital (portfolio, direct, and external commercial borrowing) inflows did lead to an appreciation of the exchange rate, and therefore a long-run co-integrating relationship is found to exist between with the real effective exchange rate and capital

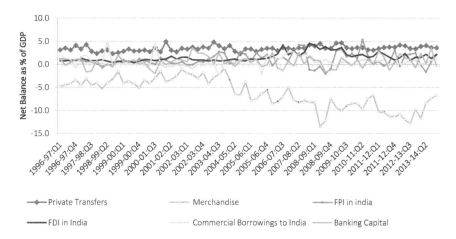

Figure 2.7 Share of net balance of components of BoP (as % of GDP)

Source: Database on Indian Economy, RBI

flows (Dua and Sen, 2006). Consequently, volatility in exchange rate too is driven by the fluctuations in capital flows (Goyal, 2012).

It is worth examining, therefore, if in recent times the exchange rate continues to be affected by fluctuations in the items of the external account, particularly capital flows.

Many factors, such as government spending, openness of external account capital flows, and net foreign assets, are shown to influence movements in Real Exchange Rate (RER). For example, Kumar (2010) considers whether productivity differentials (Balassa-Samuelson effect), capital flows, net foreign assets (NFA), government spending, terms of trade, and external openness have an impact on the real exchange rate in India. The study uses bilateral exchange rate, since 80 per cent of the trade was invoiced in dollars, and productivity growth, measured by the difference in GDP growth rates between India and the United States (US, USA), the study finds that the real exchange rate and aforementioned variables have a long-run relationship in the period 1997 to 2009. Differential growth rate, NFA, and terms of trade all have a significant and negative relationship with RER, and openness has a positive relationship. In another study, Patel and Srivastava (1997) estimated the long-run relationship of the real exchange rate with seigniorage[10] (% of GDP), investment-GDP ratio, import tariff, foreign capital inflow (% of GDP), and terms of trade using the two-step procedure by Johanson co-integrating relationship for the period 1960–61 to 1995–96. That is, the RER appreciates with an increase in capital inflows and an increase in protection. Dua and Sen (2006) used VAR to explain whether the real effective exchange rate is explained by the total capital inflows, volatility of inflows, money supply, real government expenditure, and real current account surplus for the period 1993 Q2 to 2004 Q1. They found that all the variables selected Granger cause the real effective exchange rate.

One common explanation for exchange rate fluctuations across studies, restricted to the early 2000s, is capital flows. It is therefore important to re-examine this in the current context. Establishing that the capital flows, and the largest component within those portfolio flows, drive exchange rate movement allow us to pre-empt the nature and volume of intervention that may be necessary if in fact the adverse movements in the value of rupee yield no material benefit to trade.

Taking the various components of balance of payments, their causal relationship with exchange rate is ascertained for the period 1993–94 Q2 to 2013–14 Q4.[11] Further, unlike the previous studies that have tended to club all components of capital inflows, the various components of capital inflows are separated because the underlying trends for each of these are different and the motives or incentives for each of these are also distinct.

Given the relative significance of merchandise trade, portfolio flows, FDI, and remittances, it is expected that these would have a bearing on the movements of the exchange rate. In order to validate whether the change[12] in each of these has an impact on the change in the exchange rate, causality is established for each of the items of balance of payments. Adopting the standard statistical practice of taking each of the variables, i.e. the exchange rate and the net balances of all components as growth rates and testing for stationarity, it is found that all of these variables are I(0). That is, they are stationary of the same order. Thereafter, selecting the appropriate length of lag[13] would be between a change in a variable and its impact on the dependent variable. A keen observer of the trends in movements in exchange rate and components of the external account would suggest that the direction of causality may run either way. That is, portfolio investments may factor in changes in exchange rate or vice versa. Therefore, in addition to determining whether certain components are related to the exchange rate, Granger causality is used to also show in which direction this impact would be. Further, since the general or overall trends in the value INR versus major currencies is the focal point of this chapter, the analysis herein uses the trade weighted effective exchange rate.

The test for bi-causality, reported in Table 2.1, shows that the real effective exchange rate for the period 1993–94 Q2 to 2013–14 Q4 responds to

Table 2.1 Granger causality for BoP items and real effective exchange rate, 1993–94 Q1 to 2013–14 Q4

Pairwise Granger causality tests

Sample: 1993 Q2, 2013 Q4
Lags: 6

Null Hypothesis:	Obs	F-Statistic	Prob.
D(MERCHANDISE) does not Granger Cause D(REER)	76	0.63360	0.7028
D(REER) does not Granger Cause D(MERCHANDISE)		0.30821	0.9304
D(FDI_IN_INDIA) does not Granger Cause D(REER)	76	0.76782	0.5980
D(REER) does not Granger Cause D(FDI_IN_INDIA)		1.39594	0.2303
D(FPI_IN_INDIA) does not Granger Cause D(REER)	76	6.55265	2.E-05
D(REER) does not Granger Cause D(FPI_IN_INDIA)		1.71671	0.1317
D(COMMERCIAL_BORROWINGS_TO) does not Granger Cause D(REER)	76	0.22243	0.9681
D(REER) does not Granger Cause D(COMMERCIAL_BORROWINGS_TO)		0.26016	0.9533
D(FOREIGN_EXCHANGE_RESERVE) does not Granger Cause D(REER)	76	3.18294	0.0086
D(REER) does not Granger Cause D(FOREIGN_EXCHANGE_RESERVE)		2.01317	0.0770
D(PRIVATE_TRANSFERS) does not Granger Cause D(REER)	76	0.97749	0.4480
D(REER) does not Granger Cause D(PRIVATE_TRANSFERS)		0.64457	0.6942

Source: All tables are estimated based on author's fieldwork unless otherwise mentioned.

growth in net foreign portfolio flows to India. No other component of the external account has a significant bearing on fluctuations in the effective exchange rate. This can be inferred from reported probability or p-values in the last column of Table 2.1. The change in foreign exchange reserves, on the other hand, has a two-way causal relationship with the exchange rate. The two-way causality can be attributed to RBI's response to stabilise the exchange rate during the periods of pronounced depreciation as well as the adverse movements in overall balance of payments position. Therefore, changes in the exchange rate tend to influence the changes in foreign exchange reserves that are used by the RBI to intervene in the market to stabilise the value of the rupee. This, in turn, has a direct impact on the value of the exchange rate.

Findings that exchange rate movements result from net portfolio flows, whereas merchandise trade has no causal relationship, are the first step in the detailed analysis that this book proposes to undertake. The exchange rate is driven by certain factors such as the portfolio investment, is the consideration for rate management, and is therefore useful for design of policy. However, the focal point of this research is that, with the changes in exchange rate, a dynamic process of adjustment, in the external account and the economy, may be set in motion. Theoretically, two kinds of adjustment ensue – price and quantity. These have been debated widely, and evidence has not been consistently presented for India. Therefore, from here on, detailed evidence will be presented on price movement and quantity adjustments in response to exchange rate movements.

Price adjustments in India: theory and evidence

In theory, the changes in the nominal exchange rate lead to an accommodating change in relative prices. On this basis, the purchasing power theory or the law of one price posits a constant real exchange rate. However, price rigidities in markets and productivity differentials among other factors could delay or negate the process of adjustment. For the period post liberalisation – that is, July 1994 to June 2014 – strong co-movement in the nominal and real exchange rate is observed between the rate of change (month-on-month) in real and nominal effective exchange rates. However, such co-movement attenuated for the period August 2012 to April 2013, when the real exchange rate appreciated despite the nominal exchange rate depreciation. The main reason for this divergence was a contemporaneous decline in global price levels and a rise in domestic prices in India (Bhagwati et al., 2015).

Nevertheless, co-movement in the real and nominal exchange rates indicates that relative prices for a small country – or more precisely, the domestic prices – do not move along with the exchange rate. Having said that, the

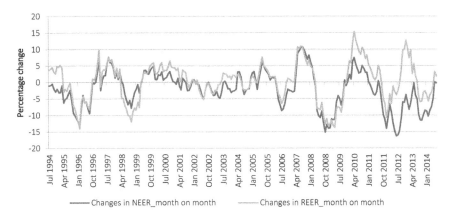

Figure 2.8 Changes in nominal effective exchange rate and real effective exchange rate (YoY), July 1994 to March 2014

Source: Computed from RBI

co-movement cannot be construed as causation. Figure 2.8 does not allow us to conclude anything about adjustment of relative prices. To move a step forward, a more formal approach is adopted to validate that domestic prices in fact do not adjust to changes in exchange rate. This is presented in the next section.

Evidence of exchange rate pass through in India

The role of the exchange rate as an instrument for adjustment in exports and imports depends on the degree of responsiveness of prices to a change in the exchange rate. The argument that exchange rate devaluation would result in higher exports because of lower foreign prices of exports and lower imports due to their higher prices assumes that an exchange rate change translates into a change in relative prices of exports denominated in dollars and imports denominated in domestic currency (or rupees). The commonly used method to estimate the impact of exchange rate on relative prices is to evaluate whether there is any exchange rate pass through (ERPT) in domestic prices.

ERPT is defined as the percentage change in domestic price as a result of a unit change in the exchange rate. A full pass through would mean that a 1 per cent change in the exchange rate would lead to a 1 per cent change in the prices. Empirical studies for India in the 1990s showed that of the entire change in the exchange rate, only 43 per cent of the total was passed on by the exporters in the form of lower export prices in foreign currency (Patra and Pattanaik, 1994).

More recent studies, such as Bhattacharya et al. (2008), found that long-run pass through in Wholesale Price Index (WPI) was only 28.6 per cent.

While the standard practice is to estimate the pass through to domestic prices, the adjustment in the external account due to change in the currency value is expected to result from the changes in prices of tradables. Studies have looked at this pass through separately. For example, Patra and Pattanaik (1994) showed that the exchange rate pass through for 1970 to 1992–3 was 57 per cent in export prices and 100 per cent in import prices. Subsequent literature relating to the decade following liberalisation has shown strong evidence in favour of incomplete pass through. For example, recent studies such as Roy and Pyne (2011) found incomplete pass through in India's export prices. The direct impact of an exchange rate movement is that it alters the existing price of tradables. A more significant impact would be when it affects the domestic prices, consisting of prices of goods other than tradables. It is seen that in the literature, both kinds of impact have been described and examined for India. This book brings together the two sets of evidence for India, for the period post liberalisation. The availability of information limits the analysis to the period 1996 Q2 to 2013 Q4. Falling in line with the commonly adopted practice in the field, pass through to domestic prices is estimated using a VAR model based on a simultaneous equations.

The measure of domestic prices used in the analysis is the wholesale price index (all commodities). It is understood that the domestic prices do not respond to exchange rate in isolation, and there are other important factors that have a bearing on domestic prices. World crude price, world food price, and the effective exchange rate, for example, all play a crucial role. To anyone familiar with the Indian economy, relevance of crude prices is well known. Crude oil constitutes the largest component of India's import basket (34 per cent in 2012–13) and is an important item of consumption as input as well as end-use. The Indian government subsidises the price of petroleum, so the pass through may be incomplete/partial; even then, world crude price movements exert significant pressure on domestic prices. The world price of Brent crude (US$ per barrel) is one of the factors that influence domestic prices.

A relatively less known fact is that the category of oil imports includes those of edible oil. In fact, India is one the largest importers of edible oil and, in 2007–08, such imports surpassed domestic production. Food items are another category of tradables, i.e. imports and exports, that are sensitive to movement in global prices. Global food prices are hence introduced in the pass through equation.

Last, to verify if exchange rate movements lead to domestic price adjustments, NEER as well as the bilateral exchange rate vis-à-vis the US dollar have been used in separate equations to estimate pass through. Usually, the nominal exchange rate vis-à-vis the US dollar is used to estimate the pass through. However, it may worth examining if the same holds true for the trade weighted effective exchange rate. This chapter presents estimates that modify the existing methods by also estimating the equation for pass through using the effective exchange rate. This is to show that the prices adjust in response not only to the major currency of invoicing, but also to that of various trading partners.

The estimation has been carried out methodically by first ascertaining whether the log(NEER)/log(NER), log(world crude prices), log(WPI – all commodities) and log(world food prices) are stationary. Note that the seasonal components of these variables have been removed.[14] It is observed that the first difference of all these variables is stationary. Then, a VAR model is estimated for the first difference of the selected variables. The estimated model allows us to verify to what extent the variance in WPI is explained by the selected variables. The variance decomposition of the changes in WPI presented in Tables 2.2 and 2.3 suggest that the changes in the exchange rate, be it the effective rate or that vis-à-vis the US dollar, explain very little of the total variation, even though the proportion of variance explained by the effective exchange rate is relatively higher. In conclusion, the price adjustment that is proposed in some theoretical arguments does not find empirical corroboration. Instead an incomplete pass through hypothesis still finds support. Table 2.2 summarises the results of variance decomposition based on the VAR performed for the period 1996 Q2 to 2014 Q2 for India. For ease of interpretation, as we move further away from the period of initial shock, less than a sixth of the variance in the domestic prices is explained by changes in exchange rate.

Table 2.2 Variance decomposition of WPI using nominal exchange rate

Period	S.E.	D(LCRUDE_D11)	D(LFOOD_D11)	D(LER)	D(LWPI_D11)
1	0.048759	10.68113	17.64467	0.108982	71.56522
2	0.055485	22.43437	22.66952	2.789138	52.10697
3	0.060086	21.53896	21.55372	8.700038	48.20729
4	0.061091	20.23571	20.16115	13.73965	45.86348
5	0.061273	20.34081	20.12787	14.30208	45.22924
6	0.061433	20.40604	20.17018	14.29450	45.12928
7	0.061490	20.36409	20.12949	14.43999	45.06642
8	0.061498	20.35667	20.11832	14.48814	45.03687
9	0.061502	20.36045	20.12045	14.48760	45.03150
10	0.061505	20.35994	20.11992	14.49028	45.02987

Cholesky Ordering: D(LCRUDE_D11) D(LFOOD_D11) D(LER) D(LWPI_D11)

Note: D(LCRUDE_D11) is the deseasonalised changes in crude prices, D(LFOOD_D11) is deseasonalised changes in world food prices, D(LAGRI_D11) is deseasonalised agricultural production, D(LER_D11) is deseasonalised nominal exchange rate and D(LWPI_D11) is deseasonalised WPI

Table 2.3 Variance decomposition of WPI using nominal effective exchange rate

Period	S.E.	D(LCRUDE_D11)	D(LFOOD_D11)	D(LNEER)	D(LWPI_D11)
1	0.051655	4.737482	4.097100	18.56545	72.59997
2	0.059022	20.98240	12.30286	18.48096	48.23378
3	0.060549	21.91537	14.18534	16.54353	47.35575
4	0.061163	21.49219	13.90706	16.77911	47.82164
5	0.061402	21.84722	13.96008	16.83052	47.36218
6	0.061456	21.90458	14.01770	16.76825	47.30946
7	0.061477	21.88667	14.00950	16.77321	47.33062
8	0.061485	21.89750	14.01021	16.77627	47.31601
9	0.061487	21.90032	14.01246	16.77410	47.31312
10	0.061488	21.89964	14.01226	16.77413	47.31397

Cholesky Ordering: D(LCRUDE_D11) D(LFOOD_D11) D(LNEER) D(LWPI_D11)

Note: D(LCRUDE_D11) is the deseasonalised changes in crude prices, D(LFOOD_D11) is deseasonalised changes in world food prices, D(LAGRI_D11) is deseasonalised agricultural production, D(LER_D11) is deseasonalised exchange rate, and D(LWPI_D11) is deseasonalised WPI

These results can be presented diagrammatically. The impulse response (IR) functions based on the estimated VAR (Figure 2.9) show that an increase in world crude prices and world food prices tends to lead to a rise in domestic prices.

Depreciation of the exchange rate leads to an immediate increase in prices followed by a reversal in the subsequent periods. Such an increase in price is expected with a rise in the price of imports upon depreciation and the impact of rise in demand for exports. While the prices do respond to changes in the exchange rate, as shown by the IR functions, the variance decomposition shows that the exchange rate explains only 18 per cent of the variance in prices. The impulse response functions show that the exchange rate has the expected direction of impact on domestic prices, i.e. an appreciation leads to lower domestic prices. However, the general depreciation of the rupee against the currencies of its major trading partners as well as the US dollar explains a fraction of the variation in domestic prices. The strong co-movement that is observed between the real and nominal effective exchange rate can be attributed to this weak pass through.

The pass through to WPI is the impact measured across a set of commodities, some of which may not be traded. Thus, the prices that are of relative importance to the present analysis are of goods traded by India. The price of goods that India exports and imports are computed using the value and volume of trade. Therefore, the partial correlation between exchange rate and price of tradables is estimated. The annual unit values

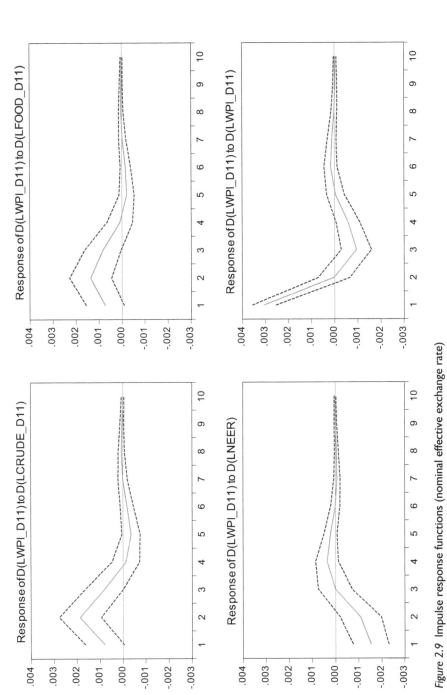

Figure 2.9 Impulse response functions (nominal effective exchange rate)

Source: Estimated

are taken for exports and imports reported by the Directorate General of Commercial Intelligence and Statistics for the period available 1975–76 to 2013–14.

The annual values of tradables are predicted using the nominal effective exchange rate, along with controlling for demand using world GDP for exports and India's GDP for imports. The predicted equations are used to find the correlation between exchange rate and unit values. Figures 2.10 and 2.11 show that the predicted value for unit value of exports (imports) controlling for world GDP (India's GDP) have a negative relationship with the exchange rate, suggesting that exchange rate appreciation leads to lower unit value of exports/imports (expressed in rupees) and vice versa.[15] The estimated coefficient for the exchange rate in the OLS is reported in Figures 2.11 and 2.12. The results are suggestive of a less than full pass through to imports (0.76) and to exports (0.71).

The analysis of the degree of correspondence between the nominal exchange rates and prices is insightful. The domestic prices show a weak or partial response to changes in exchange rate. However, for the unit value of exports and imports, expressed in INR, this impact seems to be relatively

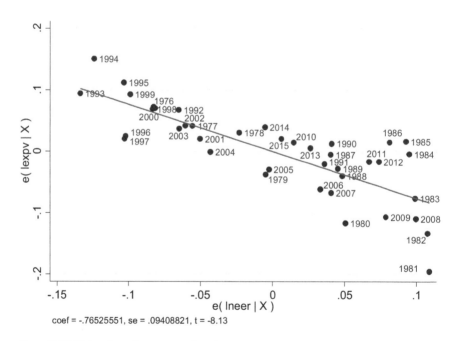

coef = -.76525551, se = .09408821, t = -8.13

Figure 2.10 Unit value of exports and exchange rate

Source: Estimated by author using an econometric model

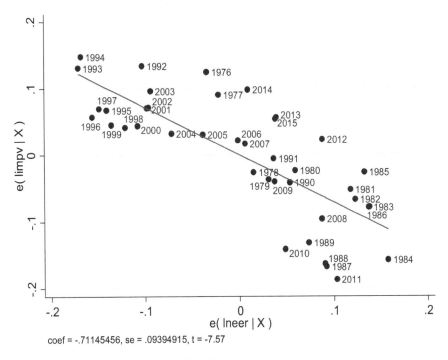

coef = -.71145456, se = .09394915, t = -7.57

Figure 2.11 Unit value of imports and exchange rate

Source: Estimated by author using an econometric model

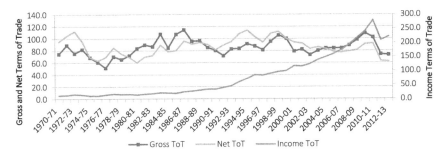

Figure 2.12 Net, gross, and income terms of trade

Source: DGCIS

pronounced. That is, following an appreciation (depreciation), the rupee value of tradables declines (increases). In sum, the prices do not adjust as expected to exchange rate movements, and this should bring about some adjustment in the trade balance through quantity adjustment.

Price and quantity changes in India's trade

Overall terms of trade

Trade deficits result from the complex interaction between changes in exchange rates, prices, and volume or quantum of trade. The empirics, as shown earlier, support limited price adjustment. A result of this unit value of tradables, expressed in domestic currency, is changes in response to changes in the exchange rate. To say that merchandise trade responds to exchange rate changes, it must be determined whether any statistical evidence suggests movements in quantity of exports and/or imports in response to the changes in the unit values. The terms of trade provide a rather simple representation of the price-quantity movements. Historically different measures evolved and were subsequently used to present the state of the economy's purchasing power.

The measure first used in the literature was the net terms of trade (NToT). It is the relative prices of exports (P^x) as compared to its imports (P^m), i.e. $\text{NToT} = \dfrac{P^x}{P^m}$. Later, Taussig (1927) recommended considering not just the prices but the *real* value of country's exports (Q^x), as a percentage of *real* value of its imports (Q^m) Subsequently, Dorrance (1948) pointed out the limitations of the net and gross terms of trade, $\left(\dfrac{Q^m}{Q^x}\right)$, and suggested an alternative that "the export value index should be divided by the import price index. The result would be an index which would reflect, for the country concerned, changes in the volume of imports obtainable from its export income" (Dorrance, 1948). Therefore, another measure was introduced, which is the income terms of trade (IToT) $\dfrac{P^x.Q^x}{P^m}$. Income terms of trade introduce quantity to the net terms of trade.

Work on India's terms of trade has been largely been confined to the period up to the 1970s. Among the first, Qureishy (1962) showed that terms of trade for Indian exports during 1951–60 deteriorated. Chishti and Bhattacharya (1976) showed that for the period 1973–75, the terms of trade for India deteriorated on account of volatile export prices, not just for primary commodities but also for manufactured items – textiles, fabrics, leather, and cotton. Dikshit[16] (2002) concluded that for the period 1957–58 to 1994–95, the terms of trade for India displayed a declining secular trend, and this was attributable to and reflective of "a number of factors working in the world economy."[17]

Not much has changed in this regard, as will be shown in this section. In the period following liberalisation, the net terms of trade have shown a decline, and in the recent period, this is observed even for India's trade in manufactured products. The movements in the net terms of trade can be divided into three phases. In the first phase, 1970–81, the net terms of trade declined; in the following decade, 1981–94, the terms of trade improved; with a reversal in this trend thereafter. The deterioration in the net terms of trade during the 1970s is attributed to the worldwide inflation (Bhattacharya and Chishti, 1976)[18] following the oil price shocks during the 1970s along with volatile export prices (Bhattacharya and Chishti, 1976).[19] In the years following 1980 up to 1998, the increase in the net terms of trade was due to the substantial decline in world gold prices and crude oil spot prices that halved over the decade. The third phase of decline was conversely because of the firming up of crude prices following the Iraq war. Therefore, oil, which contributes a large fraction to the import bill, has significant impact on the net terms of trade. A rise in the world crude prices raise the unit value index of imports thereby worsening the terms of trade. The aforementioned trend is borne out by Figure 2.13. As is evident, in the years when the oil prices went through a sharp increase the terms of trade deteriorated,[20] and vice versa. However, the relationship between the terms of trade (net) and the other significant import commodity – world prices of gold – is tenuous.[21] Only in some years such as 1997–98 and 2011–12, was the inverse movement pronounced or easily discernible. This could be because the gold imported is also used for the exports of gems and jewellery, which means that the increase in world price of gold also feeds into the export value index. However, years of weak global demand accompanied by sharp increases in gold prices were met with a deterioration of net terms of trade. Therefore, price movements are also associated with the fluctuations in specific or major commodity prices.

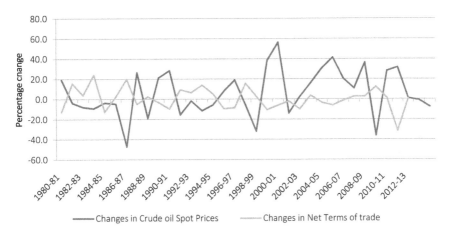

Figure 2.13 Percentage change in net terms of trade and crude oil prices (spot average)

Source: DGCI&S and GEM data, World Bank

Other than gold and oil, the other major component of exports and imports are manufactured products. During 2000–14, the unit value of imports of organic chemicals and machinery and transport equipment increased. This was accompanied by a simultaneous increase in the unit value of exports for major commodities such as iron ore, rice, engineering goods, and chemicals. However, the unit value of exports for these commodities increased at a relatively slower rate than that of import prices,[22] thus explaining further the decline in the net terms of trade.

For the gross terms of trade, there were only two discernible phases of increase: one during the decade 1976–86, and the other over the period 2002–09. During the latter period 2002–09, the quantity of exports picked up, and this increase could be attributed to the rising demand for engineering goods in East Asia and China along with an increase in gems and jewellery exports to the USA and Europe.[23] However, during the same phase, there was an expansion in imports and, as will be shown in Section 2.6, a rise in the import intensity of exports.

During these two phases (1976–86 and 2002–09) when the relative quantum of imports increased, the relative prices of exports also worsened. The opposite movement observed between the gross and net terms of trade was largely attributable to movements in imports. Therefore, there is some response to price.

During the period 2000–14, the composition of India's trade has gone through a change. Oil gained share in both exports and imports. As compared to the average of 1.5 per cent share in exports and 23 per cent share in imports during the 1990s, the share of oil in exports and imports rose to 13 per cent and 30 per cent respectively. From disaggregated trade data, it is observed that items such as mineral fuels and oil (HS code 27) that contributed less than 1 per cent in 1997–98 to total exports contributed as much as one-fifth to total exports in 2014–15. On the other hand, items of apparel and cotton (HS codes 52, 61, 73) that had contributed close to one-fifth of exports in 1997–98 are now less than a tenth of total exports. Such structural changes are bound to have an impact on the terms of trade, net as well as gross.

DGCIS provides information on the quantity and value of trade. Using that information at the lowest level of disaggregation (two digits), the weighted unit price of exports can be constructed.[24] Therefore, the value of exports for each commodity is divided by the quantity of exports, and likewise for imports. These unit values are then weighted by their share in total exports and imports to get a weighted value of exports and imports. Then the net terms of trade are calculated by taking $\dfrac{P^x}{P^m}$ for the period 1997–98 to 2014–15. Figure 2.14 is a plot of the weighted terms of trade overall as well as for manufacturing, computed using the information from DGCIS. From this plot, it can be observed that the general trend was that of deterioration of net terms of trade over the period, with the exception of minor

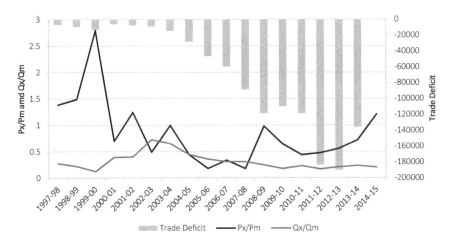

Figure 2.14 Net terms of trade, gross terms of trade, and trade deficit (in US$ millions)

Source: DGCIS (the terms of trade have been computed)

recoveries in specific years. In fact, the worsening of the net terms of trade was accompanied by an increase in the trade deficit. This could be attributed to the simultaneous increase in relative quantity of imports in the period following 2004–05. While in the years preceding 2004–05, the relative price and quantity of exports fluctuated in the same direction, post 2004–05 the two moved in opposite directions, indicating that India was losing on both counts: increasing relative quantity of imports and declining relative prices of exports. Therefore, in the years following 2004–05, the trade deficit also widened. Although there has been some improvement in the net terms of trade after 2010–11, the relatively fast increase in imports has resulted in a wider deficit.

Manufacturing terms of trade

Given that weighted unit values of exports and imports consist of commodities such as oil and gold, it is important to examine the movements in terms of trade for purely manufactures. India's terms of trade for manufactures is constructed by excluding items such as mineral oils and precious metals (HS code 27 and 71 respectively) as well as all primary commodities. Taking the weighted average prices and quantity, we see that post 1999–2000, the manufacturing net terms of trade declined or remained stagnant, implying a decline in the relative unit value of exports. This trend continued till 2006–07, followed by a rise in the net terms of trade in the subsequent years. On the other hand, there was a continued expansion in the quantity

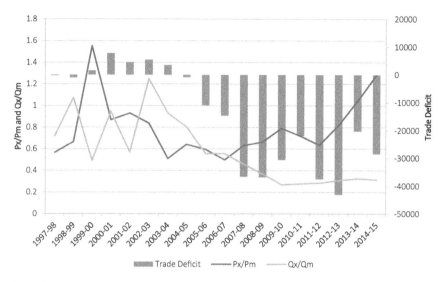

Figure 2.15 Net and gross terms of trade in manufacturing

Source: Computed from DGCIS

of imports in the years following 2002–03. As a consequence, the trade deficit expanded. Observing the trends in the ratios Qx/Qm and Px/Pm, one finds that the two for overall trade – i.e. all commodities as well that for manufacturing – have displayed similar trends, especially post 2006. The benefits from the rise in the price of exports have been offset by the expansion in the quantity of imports, such that the trade deficit has expanded over time. The observed expansion in imports, on the other hand, is explained by the rise in import intensity in the economy. This rising quantity of imports has not augured well, leading to a higher trade deficit.

There are two key takeaways from the general analysis of price and quantity movements. One is that the relative prices are prone to shocks from changes in prices of major commodities, such as crude oil prices. The other is that the quantity adjustments are limited, and one of the identifiable causes is the continued expansion in imports.

Import intensity of exports

Imports expanded in the recent period, and this in part is considered a fallout of increased reliance on imported inputs. To demonstrate that the import intensity of exports has increased for India, information on the foreign value added of gross exports is taken for India. The OECD in its

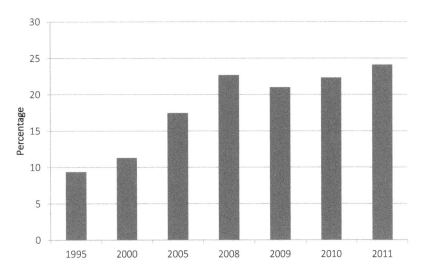

Figure 2.16 Share of domestic value added in exports (%)

Source: TiVA database, OECD

estimation of trade in value added provides information on this. The foreign value added in trade is computed by taking the input-output tables of the countries that are linked to bilateral trade to compute foreign value added. Taking the information for the period 1995 to 2011, it is observed that for India the share of foreign value added in domestic exports has increased over the period, and in 2011, it was 24 per cent. Alternatively, import intensity of exports can be estimated for production by exporting firms in India. The Centre for Monitoring Indian Economy reports information on the annual financial returns of companies in India, wherein under the foreign exchange transactions, the value of exports and imports of raw materials and capital goods is reported. First, the companies that export are selected, and only companies that report information for all years are selected for the purpose of analysis.[25]

The ratio of imported raw materials[26] to total value of sales is taken for all companies that export goods. The results for the firm level analysis corroborate those from the TiVA that import intensity has increased over time. Figure 2.17 shows that the share of imported raw materials in sales of exported companies has increased from 9 per cent in 2000–01 to 30 per cent in 2014–15. It had, in fact, peaked at 36 per cent.

Since the import intensity in production of exports has gone up over time, it is expected that the conventional expectation of exchange rate deprecia-tion being followed by a higher value of exports could be mitigated.

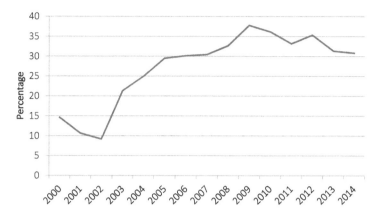

Figure 2.17 Import intensity of production of exporting units (%)

Source: Computed from PROWESS, CMIE

Exchange rate and trade

In theory, exchange rate depreciation is expected to result in an improvement in the trade balance due to the decline in the foreign price of exports and the rise in price of imports. However, this response may not be observed immediately, owed to contractual obligations in trade (Magee et al., 1974) or to a rise in import intensity where the price of exports depends on the price of imports.

Various studies for different periods have estimated the relationship of the exchange rate with India's exports and trade. Often studies show conflicting results, and the evidence largely supports a tenuous relationship between the exchange rate and trade. For example, Ghosh (1990) showed that exports measured in SDR respond to changes in world exports, GDP in agriculture, and gross capital formation, but real exchange rate has not been an important variable in influencing SDR export values during the period 1973–74 to 1986–87. Sarkar (1992) argued that exchange rate depreciation would lead to no acceleration of exports and would worsen the trade deficit. Krishnamurthy and Pundit (1995) estimated the structural model for India's exports and imports for the period 1970–71 to 1990–91 and found that "the exchange rate adjustments by themselves do not considerably change the export earnings in dollars, although they promote expansion of volume of exports as well as earnings in rupees." They found exchange rate to be an effective tool to adjust the value of imports. In a more recent study, Veeramani (2008) concluded that for the period 1960–2007, the real effective exchange rate does not bear a statistically significant relationship with exports and that the relationship between exports and REER has weakened following 2002. In a recent study, Bhattacharya and Mukherjee (2011) find that the relationship between the exchange rate and trade no longer exists once an exogenous shock is incorporated using a structural break.

The results in the previous sections show that the quantum of exports may not respond to the changes in exchange rate and that oil may drive the terms of trade. Further, the trade in oil is driven by a myriad of factors, such as domestic incentives, and that the non-oil component merits a separate analysis. Therefore, exports and imports are bifurcated into their oil and non-oil components to estimate their relationship with exchange rate for the period 1997 Q4 to 2013 Q4.

The trend in the overall exports and imports shows that the years 2002–03 and 2003–04 marked a structural shift in Indian exports and imports respectively (Figure 2.18). The faster rate of growth in exports and imports was the result of an increase in global demand for exports, particularly in Asia. On the imports side, tariff rates were brought down, and in 2003–04, the government announced its policy to align its tariff rates with those of ASEAN.[27] Further, the rise in commodity prices from 2003 contributed to the increase in value of imports. Over the 2000s, not only has the oil deficit widened, but so has the deficit for the non-oil component (Figure 2.19). The rise in import intensity of production and deterioration of terms of trade shown in the previous sections provide an explanation for the rise in the trade deficit. As Mohanty (2015) notes, India's integration with Asia, now a major region for trade, "also saw a structural increase in the import intensity of the economy as a result of dependence on hi-tech imports." The market for exports of oil has

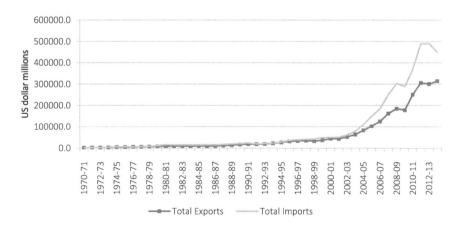

Figure 2.18 Total exports and import, 1970–2013 (in US$ millions)

Source: DGCI&S

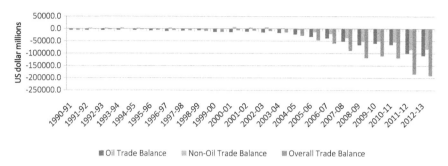

■ Oil Trade Balance   ■ Non-Oil Trade Balance   ■ Overall Trade Balance

Figure 2.19 Trade deficit (oil and non-oil, in US$ millions)

Source: DGCIS

developed largely because of various domestic incentives (such as variations in import and excise duty rates on crude and refined petroleum products) offered to firms to export.

Over the period 2004–15, there has been a creation of additional oil refining capacity in India. In 2004–05, the refining capacity was 127.4 MMT[28] while in 2015, it was reported to be 215.066 MMT.[29] Such an increase in the refining capacity, along with the change in the structure of such capacity, was among the primary causes for expansion in exports. However, it is also observed that such an expansion in exports came largely through exports of the private sector. The public sector is limited to servicing domestic demand. The wedge that appeared between domestic and world prices post 2003 contributed to the expansion in exports, as higher international oil prices that did not translate into higher domestic prices encouraged the private companies to sell abroad (Chakravarty, 2015).

Veeramani (2012) showed, using the CMIE database, that in 2010–11, 68 per cent of the exports of petroleum products was by Reliance Industries and 8 per cent by Essar Oil. The problem with the export of petroleum by India is twofold. Not only is the market concentrated, but the exports require crude oil for exports, almost all of which is sourced through imports.[30]

Reliance had exported about $31 billion in 2011–12 but it consumed $39 billion worth of imported raw materials, a major part of the latter would be crude oil. According to the United Nations Industrial Development Organisation's (UNIDO) industrial statistics, the value added to output ratio for India's refined petroleum products industry is 0.155. Applying this ratio, the value added component of India's petroleum exports in 2010–11 is approximately $6.5 billion while the gross export value, according to the official data, is as high as $42 billion.

The increasing exports by the private sector and their concentration reflect that exports of petroleum products by India are a function of global demand, growth of refining capacity of other developing countries, exchange rate and domestic prices, and world oil prices (Chakravarty, 2015).

The estimation of the equations for oil exports shows that the exchange rate and GDP have simply no impact on exports, regardless of the specification. The interesting result from the estimation is that the increase in domestic manufacturing GDP results in lower value of exports. It is often argued that oil exporting companies sell in the domestic market only when there is a slowdown in global demand.[31] Results from the analysis confirm such arguments, as estimates show oil exporting companies sell only in the domestic market when industrial demand (see the Appendix, Table 2A.3) is higher; otherwise, they prefer exporting.

To elaborate further, the expansion in export of petroleum products has occurred because of differential domestic and international prices of these products coupled with a decline in the customs duty from 20 per cent in March 2004 to 5 per cent in June 2011, and this was further brought down to zero.[32] This, along with delicensing of petroleum refining, has led to the rapid expansion of domestic refining, which was largely driven by the setting up of the Jamnagar refinery by Reliance. It is believed that Reliance exports close to 60 per cent of its output[33] with a profit margin of $12/barrel, all attributable to lower operational expenditures coupled with low costs of importation. Therefore, the exports and imports of oil are expected to be driven by corporate decisions to refine and sell in foreign markets rather than the conventional factors of foreign demand and competitiveness influenced by exchange rate.

On the other hand, oil imports display inelasticity such that an increase in crude prices and the depreciation of the exchange rate lead to higher oil import bills (see the Appendix, Table 2A.3).

India exports a wide range of items and is not a dominant supplier in any specific commodity. Thus, it is expected that with a rise in global imports, the demand for non-oil exports also increases. Non-oil exports are predicted using world imports and the REER. FII outflows, which ensued the Euro debt crisis and the weak economic outlook in 2012, caused the rupee to depreciate substantially. This sharp depreciation driven by external shocks is identifiable as a structural break in the series. Therefore, the impact of the exchange rate changes on non-oil trade is estimated, and it is further examined if this relationship has been altered following 2012.

The equation is estimated using the ARDL method which allows the inclusion of variables that are stationary of different orders. Further, the lag selection for each variable is based on the Schwarz criterion that ensures that the estimated model does not have serial correlation. The estimated equation for exports is as follows:

$$logNon-oil\ Exports = \alpha + \beta_1 logREER + \beta_1 logREER * dummy$$
$$+ \beta_3 logWorldImports + \beta_4 t \tag{2.1}$$

The estimated values are contained in Table 2.4.

The results from the regression suggest that the exchange rate does not have significant impact on the value of exports though the sign of the coefficient is as expected, i.e. depreciation leads to higher value of exports. While it is true that in the period post liberalisation, the relationship between the exports and exchange rate is tenuous, this does not hold true for the period following 2012. The pronounced depreciation of the nominal exchange rate translated into higher t export post 2012, suggesting that in periods of strong depreciation/appreciation the exchange rate can lead to higher/lower exports. Even though the nominal exchange rate depreciated in the period after 2012, the real exchange rate appreciated. This appreciation led to a sharp decline in exports as suggested by the estimated coefficient. World demand measured by world imports has a positive impact on India's exports.

Moving to non-oil imports, the previous sections described the rise in the import intensity, as was also reflected in the decline in Qx/Qm for the manufacturing sector. Therefore, the increased production of manufactures is expected to entail higher imports, and so manufacturing GDP has been taken as one the explanatory variables in addition to the exchange rate. As in the case of exports, it is useful to examine if the sharp depreciation in the period following 2012 has had any impact on import and exchange rate relationship. Therefore, an interaction dummy with the exchange rate is introduced in the estimated model.

$$logNon-oil\ Imports = \alpha + \beta_1 logREER + \beta_1 logREER * dummy$$
$$+ \beta_3 logManufacturing\ GDP + \beta_4 t \tag{2.2}$$

Table 2.4 Estimated equation for non-oil exports

Independent variable	Coefficient value	t-statistic
Log (World Imports)	0.48***	2.95
Log(REER)	−0.023	−0.069
T	.007***	4.54
C	−0.17	−.26
Dummy$_{2012}$ * REER	−0.039**	−2.16
Non-oil exports (−1)	.321**	2.5
R square		.987

Note: * implies significant at 10 %, ** implies significant at 5%, and *** implies significant at 1%

Table 2.5 Estimated equation for non-oil imports

Independent variable	Coefficient value	t-statistic
Log (manufacturing GDP)	0.935***	3.09
Log (REER)	0.543*	1.67
T	−0.004	−1.44
C	−2.11**	−2.44
$Dummy_{2010}$ * REER	−0.055**	−2.65
Non-oil imports (−1)	0.602***	6.58
R^2		.9879

Note: * implies significant at 1%, ** implies significant at 5%, and *** implies significant at 1%

From Table 2.5, it is evident that the exchange rate had a positive impact[34] on the value of imports, which means that the appreciation translated into higher value of imports. However, in the period following 2012, this impact has been only slightly mitigated. Similar to the exports, the imports are driven by demand side effects captured herein by manufacturing GDP in India. A higher manufacturing GDP leads to higher imports.

In sum, the exchange rate seems to have had little or no impact on the overall value of exports and imports in the period prior to 2012. This in fact ties in with the limited quantity adjustment, especially for exports, demonstrated in the earlier sections.

Conclusion

This chapter began by tracing the history of exchange rate management in India. As discussed, some intervention by the Reserve Bank of India is still observed during episodes of extra-ordinary volatility, or as is seen, depreciation. Despite such intervention, the value of the Indian currency has been volatile over the recent period and has been pronounced during the years following the global financial crisis. The main source of such volatility is the erratic portfolio flows.[35] Considering that there are instances of sharp depreciation, the RBI may consider the possible rationale for its intervention. Exchange rate depreciation is theoretically expected to bring about some improvement in the current account, through higher export and lower import of goods. Such impact assumes that the prices do not adjust. There is evidence that supports the latter; that is, domestic prices do not adjust following an exchange rate movement, thus leading to a one-to-one correspondence between real and nominal exchange rates. However, the unit value of exports and imports is shown to respond strongly to changes in the exchange rate. The rupee value of tradables increases with a nominal depreciation. This result is expected for unaltered domestic prices. On the flip side, quantity adjustments are limited and imports have expanded, largely due to the rise in import intensity across sectors. While analysing India's trade, it is important to consider developments such as the rapid growth in oil exports. It is shown that the exports picked up in the early 2000s with the offer of incentives. The oil imports are relatively easy to explain. Import dependency on crude is well known, and as a result the adjustments in the import bill of crude are minimal or inelastic. This trend is the outcome of various incentives offered in the domestic economy and therefore do not reflect well on India's competitiveness. Therefore, the final analysis in this chapter is carried out after bifurcating the exports and imports into their oil and non-oil components.

The estimated equations reveal that while the coefficients for the exchange rate are in the expected direction for both exports and imports, they are insignificant. Recent studies have demonstrated the lack of response (Veeramani, 2008) of exports to exchange rate changes due to various factors such as inter linkages between exports and imports (Bhanumurthy and Sharma, 2013). The empirics in this article find similar evidence for the non-oil component. As for the imports, the expected direction of impact is observed, which was evident in the movements of gross terms of trade.

An important result that emerges from the analysis is that in general, exports are driven by the world demand for exports and imports by manufacturing GDP. This suggests that demand side factors play a significant role.

To the reader it may appear that the matter is settled: the exchange does not influence exports, whereas the non-oil imports may be affected by exchange rate movements. However, when read more carefully, the results suggest that components of trade respond to different incentives and measures, as was shown through the bifurcation of trade into the oil and non-oil components. A decision to intervene in the market for exchange rates must thus be based on a more nuanced and disaggregate understanding of India's external account. Taking from the discussion in this chapter, the book develops a disaggregate analysis of India's trade, reserving the policy conclusions to be derived in the concluding chapter.

Appendix

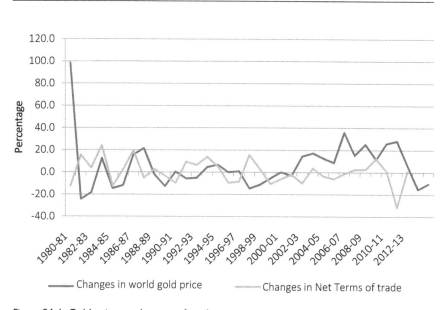

Figure 2A.1 Gold prices and terms of trade

Sources: Computed from DGIS and GEM database, World Bank

Table 2A.1 Unit value index of imports

Year	Machinery and transport equipment	Organic chemicals	Petroleum Crude
1999–00	100	100	100
2000–01	101	108	128
2001–02	104	110	128
2002–03	123	131	154
2003–04	122	139	154
2004–05	131	167	203
2005–06	138	179	286
2006–07	167	202	329
2007–08	155	192	368
2008–09	163	228	368
2009–10	148	207	328
2010–11	172	240	380
2011–12	463	288	380
2012–13	477	311	414
2013–14	608	348	447

Source: DGCIS

Table 2A.2 Unit value of exports

Year	Machinery specialised for particular industries	Textile yarn, fabrics, made-up articles, and related products	Rice	Iron ore and concentrates
1999–00	100	100	100	100
2000–01	100	100	101	115
2001–02	99	99	110	124
2002–03	98	98	112	123
2003–04	97	97	122	162
2004–05	99	103	139	271
2005–06	100	102	145	320
2006–07	104	101	151	326
2007–08	106	104	192	567
2008–09	108	106	288	561
2009–10	107	121	268	505
2010–11	117	129	239	828
2011–12	119	142	249	969
2012–13	123	145	274	979
2013–14	170	146	351	1,018

Source: DGCIS

Table 2A.3 Estimated ARDL coefficient for oil exports and imports

Log(oil exports)		Log(oil imports)	
Log oil exports (−1)	0.81***	Log oil import (−1)	0.148***
Log oil exports (−2)	−0.56	Log reer	0.48
Log oil exports (−3)	0.23	Log reer (−1)	−0.87**
logreer	5.5**	Log crude price	0.85**
logcrude	0	Log India's GDP	0.36***
logcrude(−1)	−0.64	Constant	1.254
logcrude(−2)	0.2	Trend	0.003
logcrude(−3)	1.9**		
Log GDP manufacturing	5.19		
Log GDP manufacturing (−1)	−0.56		
Log GDP manufacturing (−2)	−2.28		
Log GDP manufacturing (−3)	−7.74***		
Constant	2.43		
Trend	0.07***		
R square	0.94	R square	0.996

Source: Estimated

Note: * implies significant at 1% **, implies means significant at 5%, and *** implies means significant at 1%

Table 2A.4 Long-run coefficients of oil imports

Regressor	Coefficient	T-Ratio [Prob]
dLOGREER	0.48	1.37 [.177]
dLOGCRUDE	0.85	16.45 [.000]
dLOGGDPSA	0.36	2.58 [.013]
dC	1.25	1.66 [.102]
dT	0.003	1.28 [.204]
ecm(−1)	−0.85	−16.25 [.000]

Source: Estimated

Note: * implies significant at 1% **, implies means significant at 5%, and *** implies means significant at 1%

Notes

1 *The Economist*, "India's strong rupee," 2007.
2 The administrative controls included imposition of interest surcharge on import finance in effect from October 1995, tightening of concessionality in export credit for longer periods, and easing of CRR requirements on domestic as well as non-resident deposits from 15.0 per cent to 14.5 per cent in November 1995. Foreign currency denominated deposits like FCNR (B) and NRD were exempted from CRR requirements, and interest rates on NRE deposits were increased.
3 Such reforms included an increase in interest rate surcharge on import finance from 15 to 25 per cent, discontinuation of Post-Shipment Export Credit denominated in US dollars (PSCFC) in effect from 8 February 1996, and weekly reporting to the RBI of cancellation of forward contracts booked by ADs for amounts of US$1 million and higher. Other measures included relaxation in the inward remittance of GDR proceeds, relaxation in the external commercial borrowing (ECB) norms, freeing of interest rate on post-shipment export rupee credit for over 90 days and up to 180 days, etc.
4 Economic Survey 2012–13.
5 Mild appreciation of rupee was observed in certain quarters.
6 Rs 12000 crores in July 2013
7 The rate was increased from 8.25 per cent to 10.25 per cent.
8 This is known to be a superior measure, since it has the property that the standard deviation will equal zero if the exchange rate follows a constant trend.
9 Banking capital comprises three components: (a) foreign assets of commercial banks (ADs); (b) foreign liabilities of commercial banks (ADs), and (c) others. Foreign assets of commercial banks consist of (1) foreign currency holdings, and (2) rupee overdrafts to non-resident banks. Foreign liabilities of commercial banks consists of (1) non-resident deposits, which include receipt and redemption of various non-resident deposit schemes, and (2) liabilities other than non-resident deposits, which comprises rupee and foreign currency liabilities to non-resident banks and official and semi-official institutions. Others under banking capital include movement in balances of foreign central banks and international institutions like IBRD, IDA, ADB, IFC, IFAD, etc., maintained with RBI as well as movement in balances held abroad by the Indian embassies in London and Tokyo.
10 Seignorage/inflation tax = inflation rate $(r) \times$ real money base (M/p). The authors propose that seignorage, or inflation tax, is expected to have a negative impact on non-traded wealth. Therefore, a higher inflation tax will lead to lower demand for non-tradables, which in turn would require a higher level of RER to restore equilibrium in the non-tradables market.
11 Note that though information is available for the period prior to this, the estimation of causality has only been done post 1993–94 Q2, since in March 1993 the dual exchange rate converged, and India moved to a managed float.
12 Growth rates are taken since the variables were stationary when taken as growth rates, and the question is whether changes in one cause a change in the other.
13 Different methods were used to select the lag, and they all indicated that a quarter's lag may be most appropriate.
14 Note that if we do not de-seasonalise the crude and exchange rate data, the results remain unchanged.
15 The partial correlation plot takes the correlation between the unit value computed by taking out the impact of the GDP with the exchange rate net of the

impact of GDP. Therefore, it measures the extent to which the unit value is related to the exchange rate after taking out the correlation between GDP and each of these variables.

16 Dikshit (2002: 125).
17 Dikshit (2002: 125).
18 Dikshit (2002: 434).
19 Dikshit (2002: 434).
20 Due to the oil price shocks in the 1970s, the data for those years have been excluded.
21 See the Appendix, Figure 2A.1, for a graph.
22 See the Appendix, Tables 2A.1 and 2A.2
23 Economic Survey, 2004–05, composition of trade.
24 Note that in the computation some of the outliers were dropped. These include ships, boats, and floating objects as well as aircraft, since these are low quantity and high value items that bias the computation of unit values.
25 Some of the companies that were outliers in terms of their ratios of imports to sales were excluded from the sample.
26 If one were to take capital goods, the ratio would be much higher; however, they have been excluded because it is difficult to apportion the capital goods used in that year specifically, while for raw materials it is safe to assume the same proportion is used.
27 Economic Survey (2004–05: 115).
28 Government of India (2014).
29 Government of India (2014).
30 Veeramani (2012: 96).
31 "Petroleum product exports slip 6%," July 2015.
32 "Budget 2015: Customs duty on crude oil may be re-introduced," February 2015.
33 "India sells excess oil refining capacity to oil-parched west," 2009.
34 Although the p-value is 0.1 and the coefficient is marginally significant.
35 The coefficient of variation is (2) which is higher than that of the other significant component, that is, merchandise trade (–1).

References

Bhagwati, J., Barua, A., and Khan, M.S., 2015. Is rupee overvalued? ICRIER Working Paper No. 304 available at http://icrier.org/pdf/Working_Paper_304.pdf

Bhanumurthy, N.R. and Sharma, C., 2013. Does weak rupee matter for India's manufacturing exports? National Institute of Public Finance and Policy Working Paper No. 115.

Bhattacharya, B. and Mukherjee, J., 2002. Causal relationship between stock market and exchange rate. Foreign exchange reserves and value of trade balance: A case study for India, available at https://opendocs.ids.ac.uk/opendocs/handle/123456789/3057

Bhattacharya, R. and Mukherjee, J., 2011. Do Exchange Rates Affect Exports in India? (January 21), available at SSRN: https://ssrn.com/abstract=1744810 or http://dx.doi.org/10.2139/ssrn.1744810

Bhattacharya, R., Patnaik, I., and Shah, A., 2008. *Exchange rate pass-through in India*. Macro/Finance Group at National Institute of Public Finance and Policy, [Online] available at http://macrofinance.nipfp.org.in/PDF/BPS2008_erpt.pdf

"Budget 2015: Customs duty on crude oil may be re-introduced", February 2015 available at http://articles.economictimes.indiatimes.com/2015-02-16/news/59196846_1_customs-duty-domestic-oil-fields-domestic-crude

Chakravarty, M., 2015. India's foreign trade: Recent patterns, challenges, and prospects. In *Economics: Volume 2: India and the International Economy*. New Delhi: Oxford University Press.

Chishti, S. and Bhattacharya, B., 1976. India's terms of trade. *Economic and Political Weekly*, pp. 429–435.

Dikshit, P., 2002. *Dynamics of Indian export trade*. New Delhi: Deep and Deep Publications.

Dorrance, G.S., 1948. The income terms of trade. *The Review of Economic Studies*, 16(1), pp. 50–56.

Dua P. and Ranjan, R., 2010. Exchange rate policy and modelling in India. *RBI Development Research Group Study*, (33).

Dua, P. and Sen, P., 2006. Capital flow volatility and exchange rates: The case of India. Central for Development Economics, Department of Economics, Delhi School of Economics. Working Paper No. 144.

Economic Survey, 2004–05. "Composition of trade" available at http://indiabudget.nic.in/es2004-05/chapt2005/chap65.pdf

The Economist, "India's strong rupee", 2007 available at www.economist.com/node/9396854

Ghosh, J., 1990. Exchange rates and trade balance: Some aspects of recent Indian experience. *Economic and Political Weekly*, March 3, pp. 441–445.

Goyal, A., 2012. Evolution of India's exchange rate regime. Indira Gandhi Institute of Development Research, Mumbai Working Papers 2010–024, Indira Gandhi Institute of Development Research, Mumbai, India.

Goyal, R., Jain, R., and Tewari, S., 2013. Non deliverable forward and onshore Indian rupee market: A study on inter-linkages. *Reserve Bank of India Working Paper Series, 11*, p. 2013.

Government of India, 2014. "Indian petroleum and natural gas statistics," 2014–15, available at www.petroleum.nic.in/docs/pngstat.pdf

"India sells excess oil refining capacity to oil-parched west," 2009, available at www.thefreelibrary.com/India+sells+excess+oil+refining+capacity+to+oil-parched+west.-a0225589911

Jalan, B., 2003. Exchange rate management: An emerging consensus? *RBI Bulletin*, (47), p. 9.

Kohli, R., 2000. Aspects of exchange rate behaviour and management in India 1993–98. *Economic and Political Weekly*, pp. 365–372.

Krishnamurthy, K. and Pandit, V., 1995. India's trade flows: Alternative policy scenarios: 1995–2000, Centre for Development Economics, Delhi School of Economics, Working Paper No. 32.

Kumar, S., 2010. Determinants of real exchange rate in India: An ARDL approach. *Reserve Bank of India Occasional Papers*, 31(1), pp. 33–64.

Magee, S.P., Branson, W., and Krause, L., 1974. US import prices in the currency-contract period. *Brookings Papers on Economic Activity*, 1974(1), pp. 117–168.

Mohanty, M., 2015. India: Globalisation and growth. *IIM Calcutta Working Paper Series No. WPS-762*, Indian Institute of Management Calcutta, Kolkata, India.

Patel, U. and Srivastava, P., 1997. *The real exchange rate in India: Determinants and targeting.* Centre for Economic Performance, London School of Economics and Political Science.

Patra, M.D. and Pattanaik, S., 1994. Exchange rate pass through and the trade balance: The Indian experience. *Reserve Bank of India Occasional Papers, 15*(4), pp. 281–314.

Pattanaik, S. and Sahoo, S., 2003. The effectiveness of intervention in India: An empirical assessment. *Reserve Bank of India Occasional Papers, 22.*

"Petroleum product exports slip 6%", July 2015, available at www.livemint.com/Opinion/FhqDePOgn8aJvk9D4rYNoK/Exchange-rate-passthrough-by-Indian-and-Chinese-exporters.html

Prakash, A., 2014. Major episodes of volatility in the Indian foreign exchange market in the last two decades (1993–2013): Central bank's response. *Reserve Bank of India Occasional Papers, 33*(1 & 2).

Qureishy, I., 1962. India's Terms of Trade, 1951–1961, *Economic Political and Weekly, 14*(34), 1377–1380.

Roy, S.S. and Pyne, P.K., 2011. Exchange rate pass-through and India's export prices. *Trade and Development Review, 4*(1).

Sarkar, P., 1992. Rupee depreciation and India's external trade and payments since 1971. *Economic and Political Weekly,* pp. 1259–1266.

Tandon, S., 2014. Trade balance and the real exchange rate: An empirical analysis of multilateral and bilateral relationship. *Foreign Trade Review, 49*(2), pp. 117–139.

Taussig, Frank W. 1927. *International Trade.* New York: Macmillan.

Veeramani, C., 2008. Impact of exchange rate appreciation on India's exports. *Economic and Political Weekly,* pp.10–14.

Veeramani, C., 2012. Anatomy of India's merchandise export growth, 1993–94 to 2010–11. *Economic and Political Weekly, 47*(1), pp. 94–104.

Chapter 3

Commodity-wise trade and impact of the exchange rate

Introduction

It has been established that exchange rate movements do not impact the oil and non-oil components similarly. The differential impact on oil and non-oil components of trade compels one to ask if such divergence in response is also observed for major commodities within the non-oil category. To merely observe the aggregates and conclude decisively whether to intervene in the market for foreign exchange may be inappropriate. This chapter picks up from the earlier discussion and proceeds to examine the issue for disaggregated trade. Choosing from top commodities, this chapter traces the developments in the respective markets to finally conclude whether exchange rate movements matter for trade in these select commodities.

Changes in commodity composition of trade in India

The composition of India's trade, in terms of both exports and imports, has transformed over the last decade. Two significant changes emerge when one looks at the product composition[1] of total exports. One, exports of mineral oils or petroleum products has expanded rapidly in a decade and a half. The share of oil in exports has quadrupled during this period and is now more than one-sixth of India's exports (Table 3.1). The observed expansion in the share of exports of petroleum products by India is often argued to be on account of the combination of duties and subsidies that create perverse incentives, especially for private players. Kumar and Palit (2007) argue that

> petroleum product exports reflect neither the country's comparative advantage nor even a temporary supply surplus. These are a consequence of the rather perverse incentives built into the (formally abolished!) administered oil price regime. These have encouraged the largest refinery in India to export a major part of its output rather than supply it in the domestic market even at the cost of mothballing its retail outlets.[2]

Table 3.1 Product composition of exports (%)

Commodity	2000–1	2005–6	2010–11	2014–15
Mineral fuels	4.3	11.5	17.1	18.6
Gems and jewellery	16.7	15.4	17.5	13.4
Vehicles and parts thereof	2.1	3.2	3.7	4.7
Organic chemicals	3.9	4.7	3.6	3.9
Machinery (non-electrical)	3.2	4.1	3.6	4.4
Pharmaceutical products	2.1	2.4	2.7	3.7
Articles of clothing not knitted	8.5	5.3	2.7	3.0
Iron and steel	2.5	3.7	2.9	2.8
Electrical machinery and parts thereof	2.9	2.7	4.1	2.8
Cereals	1.7	1.6	1.3	3.1
Cotton	5.4	2.9	2.8	2.5
Articles of apparel, knitted or crocheted	4.0	3.1	2.0	2.5
Fish and crustaceans	3.1	1.4	0.9	1.7
Plastics and articles thereof	1.6	2.1	1.6	1.6
Articles of iron and steel	2.3	2.7	2.6	2.4
Meat	0.7	0.6	0.8	1.6
Aircraft and parts thereof	0.1	0.1	0.7	2.0
Ships, boats, and floating structures	0.1	0.9	1.9	1.7
Coffee, tea, and spices	1.9	0.9	0.9	0.9
Articles of leather	2.3	1.2	0.6	0.8

Source: DGCIS

The surge in the share of petroleum products in total exports, therefore, cannot be construed as a positive development.

The second major development during the same period is that the share of *traditional* exports, such as that of apparel, coffee, and leather, have more than halved. It must, however, be clarified that over the period 1995–2014, India's apparel exports have increased in absolute terms; however, the gains in the share of market have been modest. India's share of the world's apparel exports was 2.5 per cent in 1995, which increased to 3.5 per cent in 2014. However, China's, Bangladesh's, and Vietnam's shares in the world's exports more than doubled, with China contributing 37 per cent of world exports. In comparison, the increase in apparel exports by India is marginal.

With the dismantling of the textile quota regime in 2005[3] as per the WTO's agreement on textiles and clothing (ATC), India was hopeful of gaining markets that earlier had been closed to its exports. However, even now the EU, India's largest market for textile exports, imposes a duty on imports from India, whereas imports from Pakistan and Bangladesh in most cases are duty free.[4] The muted expansion in the export of apparel can be the result of such factors. An interesting development during this period has been the growth of cotton exports by India to Bangladesh, China, and Pakistan. This can be interpreted as a perverse adjustment in the structure of trade where India moved from the export of apparel to exporting cotton to the countries that offer competition to India's apparel industry.

In contrast to these two trends that signal reliance on non-traditional commodity exports, a seemingly positive development in the structure has been the growth in export of some of the manufactures. Examples include shares of organic chemicals and pharmaceuticals, as well as machinery and parts thereof in total exports.

The share of engineering goods in exports doubled to 20 per cent in 2014. Export of specific items has expanded swiftly; the share of transport equipment, for example, has tripled, from 2 per cent in the early 2000s to 7 per cent in 2014. Further, the exports of engineering goods have been subject to further diversification. Within the category of engineering goods are iron and steel (10 per cent of exports in this segment), transport equipment (28 per cent), machinery and instruments (24 per cent), and electronic goods (12 per cent). The expansion in the capacity to export engineering goods depends to a large extent on the imports.[5] Therefore, although the growth in export of manufactures is a positive development, it must be followed by the caveat that it may come with enhanced import dependence. Even for the relatively staple exports, gems and jewellery, import of raw materials such as precious stones and metals has expanded.

It may be useful to further disaggregate the composition of trade. The categories identified as top exports in Table 3.1 may be of interest. Taking four-digit classification of exports reported under these heads, it is seen that within the category of cereal exports, rice (82%) contributes a major share; the export of pharmaceuticals consists of medicaments (88%), export of gems and jewellery consisted of diamonds (58%) and jewellery made of precious metal (31%); and vehicles include motor vehicles (38%) and parts and accessories (27%), as well as motorcycles (12%). Unlike the reported categories where a single commodity forms a large part of the export, for machinery and organic chemicals, the exports are diverse.

In sharp contrast to the exports, where there has been a structural transformation as well as product diversification, the composition of imports has remained similar over the years 1990 to 2014. Six items – crude, gold and silver, precious and semi-precious stones, electronic goods, and project goods and machinery (other than electronics) – have accounted for more than two-thirds of imports over the period. The only change, also a cause for concern, is the alarming growth in the shares of crude oil, and gold and silver, in the value of imports. In fact, crude and gold account for more than a 50 per cent share in 2014–15. It is worrisome that a decline in crude prices has in no way assuaged the problem, as is seen with the expansion of oil import bill.

Other than import of oil, part of which is for the purpose of exports, India is also a major destination for polishing of diamonds and precious stones.

Therefore, the other large item of imports – pearls and precious and semi-precious stones – is an industry where imports are largely for the purpose of exports, and the value added is relatively small.[6] The major items of imports shown in Table 3.2 can be further disaggregated at the four-digit level for 2014. As is known, crude accounts for the major proportion of mineral oil imports (74%). The imports of gems and jewellery consist of two items: diamonds (32%) that are then polished and exported, and gold (55%) used for domestic consumption as well as for producing jewellery for export purposes. While it was earlier mentioned that the import basket is not as diversified, imports in the category of organic chemicals and machinery comprise a vast array of products. This may be expected, especially since there is import dependence.

Piecing together the evidence for exports and imports, one sees that there are common commodities among the top. For some categories, such as gems and jewellery, this results from import dependence for inputs. Taking the composition of exports and imports at the two-digit HS code classification, one finds that the top commodities both for exports and imports, identified as those comprising of more than 2 per cent of the total value, were in the same sectors. For example, the top five commodities for exports and imports in 2014 were in the category of mineral fuels, precious and semi-precious stones and metals, machinery, and electrical machinery. It is useful to ask whether for the top commodity segments India ran a deficit or a

Table 3.2 Share of commodities in imports (%)

Commodity	2000–01	2005–06	2010–11	2014–15
Mineral fuels	34.7	33.7	31.4	40.3
Gems and jewellery	19.2	13.9	20.8	13.0
Machinery	8.4	9.3	7.8	6.8
Electrical machinery	5.3	8.0	7.4	6.5
Organic chemicals	3.2	3.4	3.4	3.8
Plastics and articles thereof	1.3	1.7	2.0	2.2
Iron and steel	1.9	3.7	3.0	2.0
Ships, boats, and floating structures	0.7	1.8	1.0	1.5
Optical, photographic, cinematographic, and surgical instruments	1.9	1.8	1.4	1.5
Ores, slag, and ash	0.6	1.0	1.5	1.5
Fertilisers	0.9	1.1	1.7	1.2
Inorganic chemicals	2.1	1.6	1.0	1.1
Project goods	1.5	0.6	1.7	1.0
Vehicles and parts thereof	0.6	0.7	1.1	1.0
Aircrafts, spacecraft, and parts thereof	0.5	3.3	0.9	1.0
Articles of iron and steel	0.6	0.9	1.0	0.8

Source: DGCIS

surplus in 2000 and 2014. The shares of the commodities in exports and the trade deficits for each of the commodities are presented for the years 2000 and 2014 in Figures 3.1 and 3.2.

Over the decade, the shares of petroleum products and of pearls and precious stones have increased among India's exports, and this has been accompanied by rising imported content within the segment, resulting in higher trade deficits for both these commodities. While part of this can be attributed to the rise in the domestic consumption, as is the case for gold, it is nevertheless worrisome that in the product segment for which India is a major exporter, the country runs a deficit. Of the top 15 commodities that

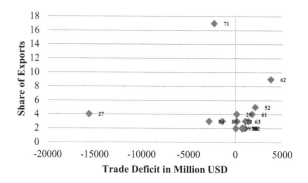

Figure 3.1 Trade deficit and share in exports in 2000–1

Source: DGCIS

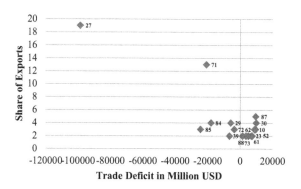

Figure 3.2 Trade deficit and share in exports in 2014–15

Source: DGCIS

Note: In the chart, the HS codes are reported as follows: 27, mineral oils, etc.; 52, cotton; 72, iron and steel; 84, nuclear reactors and machinery; 85, electrical machinery; 61, articles of apparel knitted or crocheted; 63, made up articles of textiles; 39, plastics and articles thereof; 30, pharmaceutical products; and 71, precious stones and metals.

India exports, 6 of them had trade deficits, including machinery (84 and 85). The rise in exports in these sectors has been accompanied by a relatively fast expansion in imports, such that the trade deficit in these sectors has increased. While the rise in imports of products such as machinery that has accompanied the rise in exports could be a feature of intra-industry trade, the trade deficit could also be the result of specialisation in products that are lower in the value chain and/or import dependence for production. Either way, such trends do not bode well for India's external account. The most worrying among these is the expansion in exports of petroleum products that, as mentioned earlier, have been the result of perverse incentives.

Finding support for the first factor that exports in some of India's major sectors have become largely dependent on imports, the import intensity of exports is calculated for some major sectors. The trade in value added (TiVA) database provides the domestic value added by sector and country, therefore based on their classification the foreign value added of the gross exports is reported for textiles, leather and footwear, transport equipment, coke, petroleum products, machinery and equipment, electrical machinery, and chemicals. From Figure 3.3, it can be seen that petroleum has by far the largest foreign value added, and therefore exports in this segment should be a cause for concern. It is evident from the trends that increase in exports in most segments has been accompanied by a rise in import intensity, measured by foreign value added in the major export sectors.

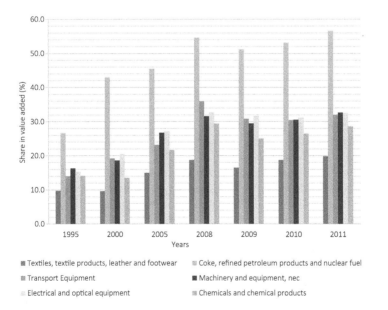

Figure 3.3 Share of foreign value added in gross exports (%)

Source: TiVA database

India's revealed comparative advantage

The prospects of trade can be evaluated in the context of the product speciali-sation and the associated import dependence. However, in the long run, trade deficits, as have been shown in the earlier section, could turn around. This is possible if India gains an advantage in the export market for these commodities.

The Ricardian theory of relative comparative advantage assumes that all other things being equal, the production of a commodity that requires a less intensive use of resources of an economy is the product for which the economy is relatively more efficient, and that should be the commodity the economy should export. However, the Heckscher–Ohlin theory postu-lates that the cost of production, as given by factor endowments and factor intensities of production, determines a country's comparative advantage. Subsequent theories of trade based on imperfect competition and increasing returns have also argued that costs of production determine comparative advantage, but in this case driven by scales of production. Therefore, to ascertain comparative advantage based on each of these theories requires the analysis of cost of production in the absence of trade and its compari-son with the costs of trading partners. To overcome this problem, Balassa (1965) introduced the concept of revealed comparative advantage, i.e. based on the composition of the trade $\frac{X_{ij}}{X_{nj}}$ where i is a country, j a commodity, and n a set of countries. Later on, this measure was modified to $\left(\frac{X_{ij}}{X_{it}}\right)/\left(\frac{X_{nj}}{X_{nt}}\right)$. The second measure computes the share of a commodity in total exports of the country relative to corresponding exports of other countries. If this is greater than 1, then the country is said to possess a comparative advantage in the commodity.

Adopting this method, the RCA for India is computed using the informa-tion on exports at the three-digit SITC level of disaggregation.[7] The market for commodities in which India possesses a revealed comparative advantage are affected not just by production condition but also by government inter-vention, changes in global production, and trade. Therefore, to be able to explain the exchange rate-trade interactions across products, a fair under-standing of the markets is requisite.

With the expansion in trade in manufacture, it may be expected that com-modities for which India possesses an advantage would consist of manufac-tures. However, studies such as Batra and Khan (2005) show that India's RCA in 2000 and 2003 was primarily in primary commodities and resource intensive manufactures. As per the study, irrespective of the level of classifi-cation (4 or 6), these two scored the highest on the RCA index. They identi-fied textile articles and chemicals (organic and inorganic) as the top sectors for which India had comparative advantage. In another study, Burange and Chadha (2008) found that the labour intensive chapters of textiles and scale intensive chapters of chemicals and iron and steel were the sectors for which India enjoyed revealed comparative advantage. Computing this for a more recent period, it is observed that, indeed, the primary commodities such as rice and cotton discernibly remain India's comparative advantage. Nevertheless, a few manufacturing products such as cinematographic films remain among the top items (Table 3.3).

It may further be useful to identify if there are commodities that now rank high among commodities for which India possesses a comparative advantage. It is observed from Table 3.4 that while there are commodities such

Table 3.3 RCA for major commodities, 2000 and 2014

Commodity	RCA in 2000	RCA in 2014
Pearls, precious and semi-precious stones	18.7	8.6
Tea and mate	17.5	4.7
Rice	14.7	17.9
Spices	14.3	9.3
Manufactures of leather, NES; saddlery and harness	14	3.2
Cinematograph films, exposed and developed	11.3	16.8
Floor coverings, etc.	11.1	6.4
Stone, sand, and gravel	9.8	5.2
Crustaceans, molluscs, and aquatic invertebrates	9.2	6.2
Textile yarn	8.3	6.4
Oil seeds and oleaginous fruits (incl. flour, NES)	8.2	2.3
Synth. organic colouring matter and colouring lakes	7.8	9.8
Cotton fabrics, woven	7.2	3.4
Iron ore and concentrates	5.7	0.4
Jewellery and articles of precious material, NES	5.7	4.9
Lime, cement, fabrics. constr. mat. (excluding glass, clay)	5.2	2.6
Other organic chemicals	5.1	2.9
Other textile fabrics, woven	4.7	1.8
Fixed vegetable fats and oils, crude, refined, fract.	4.6	0.9
Natural abrasives, NES (incl. industrial diamonds)	4.5	4.7
Household equipment of base metal, NES	4.2	1.6
Crude vegetable materials, NES	3.7	3.7
Tobacco, unmanufactured; tobacco refuse	3.6	3.3
Articles of apparel	3.9	2.1
Cotton	0.9	10.1
Vegetable textile fibres, not spun; waste of them	0.7	7
Meat of bovine animals, fresh, chilled, or frozen	2.6	5.9
Petroleum oils or bituminous minerals > 70% oil	1.3	3.8
Pig iron and spiegeleisen, sponge iron, powder and granules	2.1	3.5
Insecticides and similar products, for retail sale	3.4	3.2
Leather	3	3
Aluminium ores and concentrates (incl. alumina)	1.6	2.8
Motorcycles and cycles	1.9	2.7

Source: Computed from UNCTAD, all at SITC Rev.3

Table 3.4 India's RCA in 1995, 2000, and 2014 based on three-digit SITC code (ranks)

Commodity	2000	2014	Change
Rice	3	1	↑
Cotton	–	2	↑
Pearls, precious and semi-precious stones	1	3	↔
Spices	4	4	↔
Synth. organic colouring matter and colouring lakes	13	5	↑
Cinematograph films, exposed and developed	6	6	↑
Vegetable textile fibres, not spun; waste of them	–	7	↑
Textile yarn	11	8	↑
Natural abrasives, NES (incl. industrial diamonds)	–	9	↑
Floor coverings, etc.	7	10	↓
Meat of bovine animals, fresh, chilled or frozen	–	11	↑
Crustaceans, molluscs, and aquatic invertebrates	10	12	↔
Tea and mate	2	13	↓
Stone, sand, and gravel	8	14	↓
Made up articles, of textile materials, NES	9	15	↓
Crude vegetable materials, NES	–	16	↑
Jewellery and articles of precious material, NES	17	17	↔
Pig iron and spiegeleisen, sponge iron, powder and granules	–	18	↑
Petroleum oils or bituminous minerals > 70% oil	–	19	↑
Insecticides and similar products, for retail sale	–	20	↑
Manufactures of leather, NES; saddlery and harness	5	–	↓
Oil seeds and oleaginous fruits (incl. flour, NES)	12	–	↓
Men's or boy's clothing, of textile, knitted, crochet	14	–	↓
Cotton fabrics, woven	15	–	↓
Women's clothing, of textile fabrics	16	–	↓
Iron ore and concentrates	18	–	↓
Articles of apparel, clothing access., excluding textile	19	–	↓
Lime, cement, fabricated construction material (excluding glass, clay)	20	–	↓
Meal and flour of wheat and flour of meslin	–	–	↓
Feeding stuff for animals (no un-milled cereals)	–	–	↓
Coffee and coffee substitutes	–	–	↓

Source: Computed from UNCOMTRADE data

as rice and pearls, precious and semi-precious stones for which India has retained its comparative advantage, there are others for which India gained comparative advantage over the period – cotton, textile yarn, and synthetic organic colouring matter and colouring lakes – and there are still others, such as tea, manufactures of leather not elsewhere specified (NES), saddlery and harness, and commodities in the category of ready-made garments, in which India lost its comparative advantage.

Taking the changes in the RCA and the change in shares of India's exports between 2000 and 2014, one sees that the commodities for which India has gained significantly in terms of RCA are those for which the gains in export shares were modest. For example, cotton, cinematographic films, rice, and meat are all commodities for which the RCA increased by at least a unit; however, their shares have either increased marginally or in some cases decreased. On the other hand, with the export of petroleum products, for which the gains in RCA have been minimal, the share has substantially expanded. Therefore, the developments observed for the score on RCA is not in tandem with the changes in the structure of trade. For commodities that constitute a large part of the total exports, such as pearls and precious stones though it remains among the top commodities in terms of the absolute RCA, when one takes the change in score and the change in share, there has been a substantial decline for this category on both these counts.

Other than precious stones and metals, there are other commodities such as textile yarn and crustaceans and molluscs that still constitute a moderate share in total trade but still have low RCA scores. Last, there are commodities such as leather manufactures and tea for which the decline in RCA has been substantial, while their decline in share of exports has not been dramatic. Figure 3.4 demonstrates that the two categories of precious

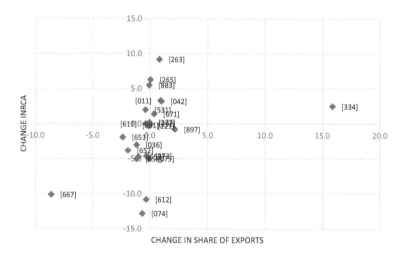

Figure 3.4 Change in RCA and share in exports of India between 2000 and 2014

Source: UNCOMTRADE

Note: 263 is cotton; 265 is vegetable textile fibres, not spun; waste of them; 883 is cinematograph films; 011 is meat of bovine animals, fresh, chilled or frozen; 042 is rice; 334 is mineral oil and petroleum products; 531 Synth. organic colouring matter and colouring lakes; 671 is pig iron and spiegeleisen, sponge iron, powder and granules; 074 is tea and mate; 611 is leather; 591 is insecticides; 612 is manufactures of leather; 667 pearls, precious and semi-precious stones, 897 is jewellery and articles of precious material, NES; and 651 is textile yarn.

stones and mineral oils are outliers, in that while the former has lost out significantly in terms of RCA and share in exports, the latter has gained in share without much gain in RCA. In order to evaluate whether the changes in other commodities were significant across the period, the same graph is presented by removing the extreme values of these two items.

Taking out the outliers, one can see that the losses in terms of share and RCA have been significant for tea and leather, while the gains on both these counts have been significant for cotton, meat, and rice (Figure 3.5).

Piecing together the structural transformation of trade and the movements in the comparative advantage merits an understanding of the underlying causes. This would in turn provide a clear picture of the global demand for products, ultimately allowing one to assess the role exchange rate can play in driving trade.

In 1995, world exports of cotton were largely sourced from countries such as the USA, Uzbekistan, and Australia; however, in 2014 India, ranked as the second largest exporter of cotton. The rise of cotton exports by India as

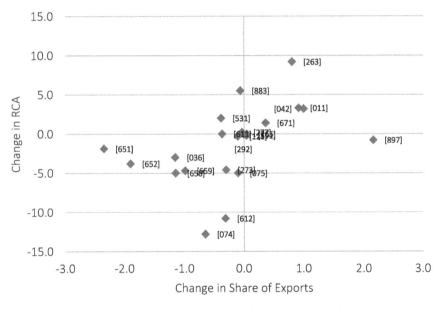

Figure 3.5 Change in RCA and share in exports of India between 2000 and 2014

Source: UNCOMTRADE

Note: 263 is cotton; 265 is vegetable textile fibres, not spun; waste of them; 883 is cinematograph films; 011 is meat of bovine animals, fresh, chilled or frozen; 042 is rice; 334 is mineral oil and petroleum products; 531 is synth. organic colouring matter and colouring lakes; 671 is pig iron and spiegeleisen, sponge iron, powder and granules; 074 is tea and mate; 611 is leather; 591 is insecticides; 612 is manufactures of leather; 667 is pearls, precious and semi-precious stones; 897 is jewellery and articles of precious material, NES; 651 is textile yarn.

well as its share in world exports has made cotton the commodity for which India possesses maximum comparative advantage. It remains to be seen how India managed to capture a large share of this market over the last decade. Pre-empting the discussion in Section 3.4, three countries – China, Bangladesh, and Vietnam – are the largest export destinations for India's cotton exports. In fact, the last decade of growth in cotton exports has coincided with an increase in exports to China. This expansion in exports has been sustained by the expansion in production of cotton that was achieved, as some argue, through the expansion of use of BT cotton crop in India that began in 2002–03 (Gandhi and Namboodiri, 2009). The increase in production, however, was overshadowed by the phenomenal expansion in exports. Domestic weavers, in fact, had to compete to procure cotton, which after its delicensing came to be dominated by middlemen who preferred to export due to the relatively favourable prices offered in foreign markets, and are often viewed as the drivers of price fluctuations (Gandhi and Crawford, 2007).

As for rice, India has always been among the top four exporters. However, over the last decade, India has gained significantly in terms of its score on RCA. India is the largest exporter of rice in the world and, as of 2014, its total share in global rice exports was 30 per cent, followed by Thailand (20%), Vietnam (10%), and Pakistan (9%), wherein Pakistan is the largest competitor to India for the exports of the basmati variety.[8] The large volume of rice exports is observed even though India consumes around 95 per cent of the rice it produces (Gulati et al., 2011). The expansion in export of rice by India has been the result of decline in the exports of its competitors – Pakistan and Thailand (Figure 3.6). The decline, post 2011, for was the

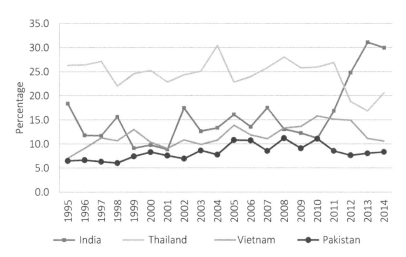

Figure 3.6 Share of countries in world rice exports, 1995–2014

Source: UNCTAD

result of the "paddy pledging scheme" wherein the farmers were given a price above 50 per cent of market price. At the same time, India has followed a "stop-go" policy with respect to the exports of rice. It is expected that since India is a dominant player in the market for rice exports, the rise in prices could potentially hurt domestic consumers. Therefore, in periods of rising global prices of rice, for concerns of food security India bans its export, as it did in 2007–08. The 2007–08 ban led to a build-up of surplus stocks of rice by Food Corporation of India (FCI). Therefore, in February 2010, exports of three varieties of non-basmati rice were allowed.

The decline in the share of Thailand rice was the result of the declining prices for its rice produce in 2013,[9] leading to stock piling; whereas Pakistan's decline in rice exports came as the result of a decline in price of basmati variety rice[10] due to lower prices charged by India which was the result of the lower Minimum Export Price (MEP). In 2012, the government lowered the MEP to gain global competitiveness.

The next commodity for which India has gained significantly in terms of RCA is meat of bovine animals (SITC 011). India rose from being 15th among the exporters of this commodity in 2000 to the fourth largest exporter of this commodity in 2014 after Australia, the USA, and Brazil. Though the share of this product in India's exports remains at 2 per cent of the total, it is a commodity that India can potentially export.[11] The market for export of this product by India consists of countries in Asia that receive more than half of the exports, the Middle East (20%), and Africa (17%). Of the Asian countries, Vietnam alone comprises (in 2014) 46 per cent of India's meat exports. It is suggested that India possessed a comparative advantage in the production of beef for a number of reasons, such as lack of commercial beef ranching, lower cost owing to cheap feed, and the provision of financial assistance to abattoirs, slaughter houses, and meat processing plants by APEDA. However, due to the shift in domestic factors, this trade is expected to be limited if not decimated.[12]

The last commodity for which India gained in terms of its score of RCA was the synthetic organic colouring matter and colouring lakes. These consist of organic dyestuffs, printing ink, synthetic brighteners, lakes, other colouring matter, glaze, enamel, driers etc., synthetic tanning substances, paints, varnishes etc., dyes, and tanning extract etc. Among other uses, this category of chemicals is used in the textile industry. In part, the cause for rise in exports of chemicals has been the shift of the production of chemicals to developing countries such as India. The low cost of production and lax regulation[13] have contributed to the rapid expansion in the market for chemicals in countries such as India and China. Further, the World Health Organisation has noted that "increased industrial and agricultural production has intensified poorer countries' production and use of both newer and older chemicals, including some formulations that are banned in other countries."[14]

Among the commodities that lost out in terms of their comparative advantage are leather manufactures. The leather industry in India has potential for growth because of the livestock that it possesses. However, as is true for the export of meat, this industry too has suffered because of the recent anti-beef movement. The predominant destinations for India's leather exports have been the developed countries. These countries have in recent times imposed strict conditions for pollution control on exports from this sector, which affect exports. In 2001, the sector, which until then was in its entirety in the small scale industry (SSI), was de-reserved for the SSI units.[15] As per the Small Industries Development Bank of India report, nearly 75 per cent of the production in 2007–08 in the leather industry was undertaken by the SSI.[16] The decline in the RCA in the segment of saddles and harness could in part be attributed to the lack of availability of good quality leather, for which India has relied on China, and the stringent conditions imposed on India by importing countries. In fact, in 2015, the European Union (EU) – India's largest market for leather exports – raised concerns with respect to the presence of hexavalent chromium[17] in the leather products. Such restrictions could further potentially harm Indian leather exports. Over the period 1995 to 2014, India's share in world exports of leather approximately halved, from 9.6 to 5.3 per cent. During the same period, China emerged as the largest exporter of leather. The shares of India and China in the world market for export of leather products have moved in opposite directions post 2000 (Figure 3.7).

The other commodity that witnessed a sharp decline in RCA was tea, even though in terms of the share of world exports, India has remained among the top three exporters of tea over the entire period. In this category, India competes with Sri Lanka and China. While India has retained its position

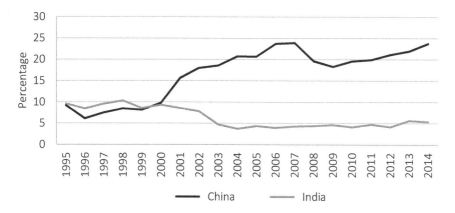

Figure 3.7 Share of exports of leather products, China and India, 1995–2014

Source: UNCTAD

as a top exporter, its share has declined over this period, from 25 per cent of the global exports of tea to only 10 per cent now. This period was also accompanied by a rise in share of exports from China, with Kenya and Sri Lanka keeping their shares largely intact. The export of tea is known to be subject to price competition; this in part is the cause identified for such a decline (Nagoor, 2009).

The major decline on both counts, as mentioned earlier, came in the segment of natural pearls and precious stones. As is known, exports of precious stones contributed 8.6 per cent of exports in 2014. India still remains the world's largest exporter of precious stones (14.5%) followed by the USA, Israel, and Belgium. However, the decline in the RCA has come about due to the competition that India faces in the market for polishing diamonds. China is now known to polish diamonds at rates that are as low as India's.[18]

Therefore, there are commodities that contribute significantly to India's exports, whereas there are commodities for which India is a lead global supplier. As is seen, these may not be the same; for example, engineering goods now form a significant fraction of India's exports, whereas when the RCA is computed, these goods do not figure among the top 20. That is, India is not yet a leader in the market for supply of such manufactures. At the same time, the commodities, largely primary, where India is a dominant exporter have been subject to shocks from both domestic regulatory shifts and global developments. Where India is a dominant supplier, the question is whether exchange rate movements can undermine its dominant position, and where India is a small fraction, it may be asked if movements in exchange rate plays a vital role in the trade of these commodities. While the regulatory changes have been documented – and these are not the only factors that drive trade – the markets, and conditions therein, to which goods are exported and from where imports are sourced also play a role. The commodity-wise trade too is analysed in terms of top countries.

Top destinations for exports and top sources of imports

Over the last decade and a half, for most commodities, the EU has remained India's major export destination.

Exports can broadly be divided into three categories: primary commodities, such as cotton and cereals; commodities that rely heavily on the import of goods, such as gems and jewellery as well as petroleum products; and lastly, other manufactures. Be it apparel, chemicals, machinery, or iron and steel, the EU's share of exports is about one-fifth of the total. However, if the shares of individual country is estimated, then the USA has remained the single largest importer of Indian goods, despite the decline in share. On the other hand, the market for India's primary commodity exports have been developing countries. For example, the market for India's cereals or rice exports consists of countries such as Bangladesh and the Middle East with Saudi Arabia and Iran accounting for approximately 26 per cent of all exports in 2014–15. Cotton exports are predominantly to China, followed by Bangladesh and Vietnam. Since these three are large exporters of apparel, they are an important source of demand. Because apparel is an important component of India's exports the rise in the value and share of export of cotton in total exports of India, whereby India supplies cotton to other apparel exporting countries, cannot be interpreted as a sign of progress. As was mentioned earlier, some of these exports compete with the domestic weaving industry. In fact, in 2014–15, the three countries together accounted for more than 50 per cent of India's export of cotton. In the exports of meats, too, one finds that the major market for these exports is the Asian region, wherein Vietnam received 46 per cent of our exports in 2015. Observing the trends in the exports of large primary commodities by India reveals that India relies on countries in Asia as well as the Middle East for its exports.

Moving to the export of manufactures, the USA has remained the largest consumer of India's exports of iron and steel (22.56% in 2014), machinery (15.63%), electrical machinery (14.57%), organic chemicals (13.7%), pharmaceuticals (30%), and textiles (21%), as well as vehicles, etc. (9%).

Destination for exports of major commodities

This part of the chapter familiarises the reader to the markets for India's exports as well as the source of imports. The intent of this digression is to show that underlying the commodity structure is also the composition of countries. Not only would the trade then flourish or decline with a change in conditions under which the countries trade, but it would also be affected by changes in the real exchange rates. This section, therefore, briefly presents the top countries for each category of major exports and imports.

Exports of gems and jewellery by India have been a fifth of India's total exports, and more than 80 per cent of these have been to just four countries – the USA, Hong Kong, Belgium, and United Arab Emirates (UAE). Even though in value, the export of gems and jewellery has expanded over the last decade and a half, these have expanded relatively fast for Hong Kong and UAE. Thus, the share of most other countries in gems and jewellery exports has declined over the period 2000–14, accompanied by a substantial increase in exports to Hong Kong and UAE. For these two destinations, the composition of exports varies. That is, while exports to Hong Kong consist largely of precious stones, those to UAE consist of gold, precious stones, and items of jewellery.

Much like the export of gems and jewellery, the export of cereals and cotton display concentration in terms of destinations. Nearly 50 per cent of the export of cereals has been to the Middle Eastern region, and 92 per cent of all exports were to developing countries (Table 3A.1).

Such concentration is more pronounced for export of cotton, where for the years 2000–14, three Asian countries – China, Bangladesh, and Vietnam – account for 56 per cent of these exports. Of note is that all three all are exporters of apparel. The expansion in cotton exports was backed by the expansion in domestic output of cotton, which was diverted to exports because of higher international prices. Domestic weavers were left to compete and had to procure cotton at high prices (Gandhi and Crawford, 2007).

With the exception of the aforementioned item of exports, all other items are exported to a variety of destinations. Take, for example, India's machinery exports, which can be divided into electrical and non-electrical. For non-electrical machinery, the USA has the largest share among all countries, and its share has remained constant over time. India exports non-electrical machinery to many countries, and 25 countries account for three-fourths of exports (Table 3A.2). In terms of major destinations, during the period 2000–14, there was a change in the composition of countries to which India exports this commodity. Between 2000 and 2014, the share of exports to developing countries remained around 55 per cent; however, within the category of developing countries, the share of exports going to the developing Asian countries and Africa declined while the share going to the Middle East increased. Within developing Asia, exports to China are an exception to the observed trend, since these have increased in terms of both share and value of exports.

Similarly, the exports of electrical machinery is not concentrated in terms of the destinations. Twenty-two countries account for 70 per cent of all exports. Further, the USA remains the single largest destination, followed by UAE. Even for this category of machinery, China has emerged as one of the top export destinations. Again, the share of developing countries has increased over time from 46 per cent to 54 per cent, of which the share of Asian countries has declined (from 31.4% to 22%) accompanied by a simultaneous increase in exports to Africa and the Middle East (Table 3A.3).

Vehicles and parts also are exported to many countries, with the USA retaining the largest share among these. However, unlike machinery where developing countries, particularly those in the Middle East, account for a large share, a third of the exports are to OECD countries. Africa has become another important destination. In 2014, African countries received 14 per cent of the exports (Table 3A.4).

Unlike other products where the share of exports to the USA has declined, there has been a massive increase in the US share of pharmaceutical exports. Over the period 2000–14 it increased fivefold. This was accompanied by a decline in shares of exports to Russia and Kenya. The phenomenal increase in exports to the USA may be explained by the rapid expansion intra-MNC trade. This is turn has flourished after the shift in patent regime in India from process to product patent based. There has also been substantial growth in the M&As in this industry. Therefore, exports to the USA can be viewed as a measure of trade by MNCs that have set up shop in India to tap into developing country markets,[19] including for the purpose of intra-company by those headquartered in developed countries. Just as for the export of vehicles, Africa is an important market for exports of pharmaceuticals. The countries from Africa among the top 20 comprise 15 per cent of all exports (Table 3A.5).

The USA and China remain among the top two partner countries for export of organic chemicals. As mentioned earlier, the industry shifted to developing countries since this is relatively under-regulated. As is expected, the share of developed countries in India's export of organic chemicals among the top 20 destinations is close to 45 per cent.

The export of apparel, though decreased in share, has increased in absolute terms over the period 2000–14. Among the top destinations are the USA, the EU, and UAE. However, the US share has declined due to the relatively rapid expansion of exports to the other two (Table 3A.9).

The last major export for India is petroleum products. A fifth of these were exported in 2014–15 to UAE and Saudi Arabia, which are also major sources of oil imports. The excess refining capacity created in India is utilised for processing crude that is then exported to these countries.

The regional distribution of India's exports has transformed over the period 2000–14. The share of developing countries has increased for exports of *all* commodities except pharmaceuticals and organic chemicals. The pharmaceutical sector, as was shown earlier, is the lone sector for which the US share expanded over the period of analysis. In fact, the decline in the share of developing countries was 30 per cent, which was accompanied by an expansion of exports to countries such as the USA and the UK. The growing presence of MNCs in the Indian pharmaceutical sector was also reflected in the shift from generic to formulation drugs. In the case of organic chemicals, the shares of developing countries remained the same over the period.

The expansion in trade with developing countries has been the most dramatic in the case of gems and jewellery, as their share in exports went from 34 per cent in 2000–01 to 63 per cent in 2014–15. This was largely driven by growth in exports to the Middle East and in particular to UAE. For all the major commodities reported earlier, UAE has now emerged as an important market. For most commodities, its share in exports was in excess of 5 per cent of the total.

Though the EU and the USA have remained major destinations for the export of manufactures, there has been a decline in their shares for most commodities. China has emerged as the top export destination for commodities such as cotton, machinery, and organic chemicals. Further, Africa has emerged as an important market for India's exports. For commodities such as petroleum products, pharmaceuticals, and vehicles (and parts thereof) countries from Africa have a significant share of exports.

Top sources of imports

In sharp contrast to the exports, it will be shown herein that for import of major commodities, India relies on a few countries. Take, for example, the import of gems and jewellery. These are largely concentrated, where Switzerland, Belgium, UAE, Hong Kong and the USA account for more than 70 per cent of all imports. Further breaking down imports into the subcomponents, it is seen that imports from Switzerland consist mostly of gold, whereas those from Belgium consist of precious stones.

While a different set of countries dominates the imports of ores, slag, and ash, these have remained concentrated. In 2014, 60 per cent of the import of ores was from three countries: Chile, Australia, and South Africa, replacing China, Argentina, and Bahrain as the top source of India's import of ores. Chile exported copper ore and the other two export iron ore.

For all other imports, excluding crude. China dominates as the single largest source. For example, in 2014–15 India imported 35.7 per cent of its organic chemicals, 14 per cent of inorganic chemicals, 49.4 per cent of fertilisers, 50 .5 of electrical machinery, 31.9 of non-electrical machinery and 32.7 per cent of Iron and Steel from China. There has been a visible increase in the import dependence on China (Tables 3A.11 to 3A.20).

As for the import of crude, the partner-wise disaggregation of the imports reveals that over the years 2000 to 2014, while the OPEC countries have been among the top sources of crude imports, there has been an emergence of countries such as Brazil, Venezuela, Colombia, and Angola among the large suppliers of crude to India.

Observing the trends in the partner-wise composition of the commodity-wise imports reveal the growing significance of China for import of most commodities. In fact, for products such as fertilisers, iron and steel, machinery (electrical and non-electrical) and organic chemicals, a significantly large proportion is imported from China. The import of oil is now increasingly sourced from a diverse set of countries, as countries such as Angola and Colombia have gained significantly in terms of shares and absolute values. In the precious and semi-precious stones segment, there is a high degree of concentration of source of imports, with 60 per cent of imports being sourced from three countries: Switzerland, Belgium, and UAE. For all commodities (other than inorganic chemicals), increased concentration is observed in terms of the set of countries from which the commodity is imported.

In terms of the direction of trade, there has been a significant increase in trade with developing countries. While the Middle East has seen an increase in share of exports, Asian countries have become more significant as sources of imports. Two important trends emerge from the destination-based disaggregation of the commodity-wise trade. One, India exports to many countries, whereas imports by India are relatively concentrated. Two, the share of trade with developing countries has increased over the last decade and a half. Meanwhile, exports to and imports from developed countries, including the EU, have declined in the case of most commodities. Only in the cases of apparel exports and import of vehicles and parts thereof has the EU been able to maintain its share. Although an increase in the share of trade with the developing economies is a positive feature of this period, there are developments that must be treated with caution. For example, India is a major producer of iron and steel; however, over the years India's import of iron and steel has increased. This has been the result of the supply of relatively cheaper iron and steel from China, coupled with the relatively cheaper imports of steel from Korea and Japan facilitated by the trade agreements signed with these countries. As can be seen from Table 3A.20, the share of Korea and Japan in imports rose over the period 2000–14 and that of China exhibited a phenomenal increase such that by 2014, one-third of all imports were from China. Therefore, in specific segments, the competitive advantage of China may have adversely impacted India's output and exports.

As is seen, the last decade and a half has witnessed a change in composition of trade where India has experienced a rise in share in exports of petroleum products that are now approximately 20 per cent of all exports. Among primary commodities, cotton accounts for 2.5 per cent and fish, meat, and cereals together account for 6.3 per cent of exports. When analysing the RCA, one observes that primary commodities such as rice, cotton, and spices rank among the highest. These commodities do not contribute significantly to the exports by India, but they are those in which India possesses RCA. This reflects that Indian exporters have been able to successfully capture the global market for relatively less sophisticated products, except for organic chemical dyes.

The textile sector witnessed a decline in the RCA, even while in absolute numbers the value of exports has increased. During the period of analysis, the RCA in cotton and textile yarn increased, accompanied by a decline in that for apparel. At the same time, though the value of exports increased, the share of apparel in India's exports declined significantly, from 12.5 per cent to 5.5 per cent. As was discussed earlier, the expansion in exports spurred by relatively better international prices forced domestic weavers to compete with exports to procure the raw material. The growth of middlemen facilitating exports made the situation worse. Therefore, the trends reflect the downward movement in the value chain within the textile sector. In fact, India's increasing exports of cotton to apparel exporters is a worrying development.

Labour intensive exports[20] by India, be they leather or textiles or even gems and jewellery, have been on a downward path in terms of their shares in the total exports. India was able to maintain a comparative advantage in gems and jewellery, but there was a significant decline in both leather and textiles.

The export of leather and meat has recently suffered a severe setback with the clamp down on beef. While India held a significant share of world exports of meat, it now faces the challenge of such domestic controls.

The trends detailed in this section are important since an alternate real effective exchange rate is constructed for analysis based on top countries. This is to examine whether the effective exchange rate based on 36 countries is an effective measure of exchange rate impact, or whether a commodity specific exchange rate would be a more appropriate measure.

Do exchange rates matter for trade? Overall commodity analysis

For the exports and imports of commodities, identified in Section 3.2 as the major commodities, their relationship with the exchange rate is estimated for the period 1999–2000 to 2014–15. That is the period for which the disaggregate data are available. For the purpose of estimation, the exchange rate used here is the effective rate computed by taking the top ten major trading partners for each commodity and weighting their real exchange rates with India (based on WPI) to arrive at a separate real exchange rate for each of the commodities. Further, the effective exchange rate is computed for exports and imports separately for the same commodity or product group.[21] The measure of exchange rate is $\sum_i \dfrac{\left(\dfrac{P_i}{e_i * P^*}\right) * x_i}{x_i}$, where x_i is the share of country i in the exports of a commodity by India. The index for imports is calculated using the same method wherein the share of exports is replaced by the share in imports.

The period of analysis is limited to 1999 to 2014 since the real effective exchange rate is constructed using commodity-wise country information from DGCIS. Therefore, a panel GLS[22] is undertaken where exports are categorised as labour intensive (textiles and gems and jewellery), manufacturing (chemicals, machinery, vehicles, and iron and steel) and primary/mineral based (petroleum, cotton, and cereals). On the other hand, imports have been categorised as primary/mineral based (ores), manufacturing (fertilisers, chemicals, machinery, and vehicles) and export related imports (gems and jewellery and petroleum).

The equations estimated for exports and imports are as follows-

1. $logexports = \alpha + \beta_1 logREER + \beta_2 logREER * manfdummy$
$+ \beta_3 logREER * labour\ intens\ dummy + \beta_4 logworld\ GDP$ (3.1)

2. $logimports = \alpha + \beta_1 logREER + \beta_2 logREER * manfdummy$
$+ \beta_3 logREER * export\ related + \beta_4 logIndia\ GDP$ (3.2)

Table 3.5 Estimated equation for exports and imports using panel GLS

Independent variable	Log(exports)	Log(imports)
Log REER	0.04(0.02)	−0.035(0.048)
Log REER* manufacturing dummy	−0.03(0.204)	−0.013***(0.04)
Log REER* export related imports	–	0.026(0.089)
Log REER* labour intensive dummy	−0.09***(0.028)	
Log GDP of world		
Log India's GDP	1.07***(0.04)	1.36***(0.12)
Constant	−8.07***(0.45)	−0.49(0.84)

Source: All tables are estimated based on author's fieldwork unless otherwise mentioned.

Note: * means significant at 10%, ** means significant at 5%, and *** means significant at 1%

From the estimated relationship, reported in Table 3.5, it is seen that labour intensive exports (gems and jewellery as well as textiles/apparels) are sensitive to changes in exchange rate and a depreciation of exchange rate leads to higher value of exports. Recent research has shown that labour intensive products depend on the exchange rate of the exporter whereas sectors that are a part of global production networks are sensitive to the exchange rate of the region (Thorbecke, 2011). Such results are corroborated by this study. Further, as will be shown in the product-wise results for sectors that are known to be a part of global value chains (automobile and organic chemicals), there is lack of response of exports to exchange rate. While the sign of the manufactures is the same, the estimated coefficient is insignificant. Therefore, exchange rate depreciation does not have a significant impact on the exports in the other categories, i.e. manufacturing and primary products. While this is true overall, it remains to be seen which products within manufacturing or primary products are affected by changes in exchange rate.

As for imports, the exchange rate is insignificant for most categories, except that for manufactures, inelasticity is observed. That is, with an exchange rate depreciation, the value of imports expand. The observed inelasticity can be attributed to the rise in the import intensity of exports/production.

Other than the exchange rate, changes in income tend to have positive impact on exports and imports.

Moving from these broad categories of exports and imports, a more disaggregate analysis for products within each of these categories is presented. The purpose of undertaking the panel analysis prior to the commodity specific regression is to check for robustness of the product-wise OLS that will now be presented. Table 3.6 presents the results for the

Table 3.6 Estimated value of coefficient for real exchange rate with exports and imports

Commodity	RER	
	Exports	Imports
Cereals	0.94	–
Ores, slag, and ash	–	0
Mineral fuels	0	0
Inorganic chemicals	–	0
Pharmaceuticals	–0.51	–
Organic chemicals	0.199	–0.09
Fertilisers	–	–0.05
Cotton	0	–
Gems and jewellery	–0.73	0
Iron and steel	0	–0.57
Machinery (non-electrical)	–0.16	–0.69
Electrical machinery	–0.26	0
Vehicles and parts thereof	0.16	0
Articles of apparel knitted, crocheted	–0.47	–

Note: The coefficients reported above are zero if the value is insignificant at 5% and "–" indicates that the equation was not estimated for the said sector. For results of the model, refer to the Appendix.

estimated value of exchange rate coefficient for the product-wise regression. The specification remains the same as equations 1 and 2 (see the Chapter 3 Appendix, Tables 3A.22 and 3A.23, for details).

At the start, it is worth mentioning that the real effective exchange rate was taken for the purpose of estimating the same equations; however, in all cases it turns up insignificant. Therefore, the results presented and discussed here are using the real effective exchange rate constructed on the basis of shares of top ten countries for the commodity export/import.

Table 3.6 summarises the results from the estimates. For the sake of brevity only the coefficient for the exchange rate is reported. The export of cereals bears no relationship with the exchange rate. The demand for cereals (in particular rice) was driven by domestic export policy and developments in the world market for rice. Although for most of the period there was an increase in the price and quantum of exports (Figure 3A.2), in the recent period the decline in the prices, due to the reduction in minimum export price accompanied by the release of the stocks built during the ban between 2007 and 2011, led to the increase in exports. Moreover, the reduction in the supply of rice by competing countries such as Thailand and Pakistan helped bolster India's share in the rice market. Therefore, the estimated coefficient shows that the exchange rate has a positive impact on exports of cereals. This means that with the depreciation of the rupee, the dollar value of exports contracts even as the rupee value remains unchanged.[23] Thus indicating limited or no quantity adjustment.

The export of cotton experienced a boom with the expansion of domestic production following 2002 and a simultaneous increase in the demand from countries such as China, Vietnam, and Bangladesh that are exporters of apparel. Until 2006 the price of cotton was fairly stable. However, increasing demand for cotton led to the rise in price and the unit value of exports increased (Figure 3A.5). The exchange rate is found to be insignificant. The lack of impact of the exchange rate on cotton is expected since the price of cotton[24] in India is the lowest. The competitive prices accompanied by the demand for cotton by countries such as China that have large scale demand for stock piling, domestic producers in India choose to supply to other countries. Therefore, estimated equation for exports shows that exports of cotton are not sensitive to changes in the exchange rate.

The import of fertilisers is driven by the domestic shortfall of production (Sharma and Thaker, 2011). Further, India is the world's second largest consumer of nitrogenous and phosphatic fertilisers (Gulati and Banerjee, 2015). India imports fertilisers to make up for the shortfall in domestic production. The inelasticity of demand for imports of fertilisers is reflected in the quantum of imports, which increased in spite of the rise in fertiliser prices. Given the inelasticity, it is expected that the exchange rate changes should not have any impact on the import of fertilisers. It can be seen from the estimated equation that the depreciation results only in higher value of imports of fertilisers, thereby corroborating the hypothesis of inelasticity. Further, it can be said that there is a pass through of nominal exchange rate to the import prices of fertilisers, as an exchange rate depreciation (appreciation) leads to higher (lower) import prices, with the adjustment in the quantity being minimal owed to the large subsidy that insulates the domestic price from global price movements, leaving the demand unchanged (Figure 3A.15).

The category of precious and semi-precious stones and metals comprises a large fraction of India's exports and imports. India is the seventh largest exporter of gems and jewellery in the world. The export side consists of items such as articles of precious metals as well as precious stones. In addition to stones, the major item of imports consists of gold, which to some extent is used for the purpose of household savings. The demand for gold by households has been a cause of concern since the current account deficit expanded with the rise in gold imports.

The estimated equation for exports and imports of gems and jewellery reveal that while the former are sensitive to changes in exchange rate, the latter seem to be insensitive to such changes. The gems and jewellery exports consist mainly of polished diamonds. Countries such as Belgium, Israel, and the USA, which are also centres of cutting and polishing, have witnessed a decline, while countries such as China and India now supply close to 85 per cent of polished diamonds. The low operating margins in China and Africa compete with India's exports (Bain, 2015). Therefore, it is expected that the movements in the exchange rate have an impact on the export competitiveness. The estimated equation shows that exchange rate depreciation leads to higher value of exports of gems and jewellery.

On the import side, gold, which is for domestic consumption and exports, has until recently been subject to declining rates of customs tariff. Further, the imports of materials for export of gems of jewellery that includes gold and diamonds had been exempt from tariff. Therefore, imports are affected by multiple factors – tariff, domestic demand, and global demand for India exports or gems and jewellery – and so the exchange rate seems to have no impact on changes in imports. A separate estimate for gold reveals that gold imports are inelastic to changes in the exchange rate (Table 3A.21).[25]

Export of pharmaceuticals, as shown earlier, is sourced to two kinds of countries. One set is the developed country markets such as the USA, the UK, and Russia. The three comprised 40 per cent of exports of pharmaceuticals in 2014–15. The rest of the exports are to developing countries, especially in Africa. There has been a growing presence of foreign pharmaceutical companies post 2005 in India. This may have led to higher intra-company trade which may be pre-contracted. However, since the major share of exports is of Indian companies that potentially compete with multinational pharmaceutical companies of developed countries, the exports of pharmaceuticals are expected to be price sensitive. Moreover, India exports to markets that are also important export markets for other producers of pharmaceuticals, such as the USA. For example, India and the USA both export 35 per cent of medicaments to three countries: Switzerland, Germany, and Italy. In addition, Africa constitutes a large destination for exports of pharmaceuticals; the price is an important factor that will impact exports. The period 2000–14 was one where the price of pharmaceutical exports increased, accompanied by an increase in the quantity. The price sensitivity of Indian exports of pharmaceuticals is observed for the period of analysis where the price and quantity moved in opposite directions (Figure 3A.14). India is known for the export of cost-effective generic medicines, and the estimated coefficient suggests that the exports of pharmaceutical products are sensitive to changes in the exchange rate, as depreciation leads to higher exports.

Within the manufacturing sector, the top three commodities that India exports – organic chemicals, machinery, and electrical machinery – had global export shares of less than 1 per cent for machinery and close to 3 per cent for organic chemicals in 2014. Therefore, India has a relatively small share in world exports for these commodities.

The estimated equations provide evidence that only in the case of machinery does the expected result hold. That is, the exchange rate depreciation leads to higher exports. While India exports a larger fraction now to Asian economies, its growth in share of world market has not been exceptional, and it faces competition from China (Keshari, 2012).

Factors such as the existence of inverted duty structure that make the imports of finished products within the category cheaper than the import of raw materials also affect exports in this sector.[26] The expansion in the exports of machinery was accompanied by the increase in the proportion of foreign value added in this segment. Therefore, for non-electrical machinery, quantity of imports are inelastic to changes in the exchange rate, whereas for electrical machinery, the exchange rate has no impact on imports.

For export of vehicles (and parts thereof), the obverse signs are observed for the exchange rate, i.e. an exchange rate appreciation leads to higher value of exports. As was shown, the value of exports increased over time that may have contributed to the growth in exports. The market for vehicles and parts thereof is slightly different, as shown by Table 3A.6 in terms of destinations. It consists of countries from South Asia and Africa among the top destinations as opposed to the Asian developing economies for electronic goods. Further, there have been large numbers of joint ventures (JVs) in the automobile sector. It is expected that such JVs would result in an increase in the level of pre-contracted trade, and thus the exchange rate has no impact on imports.

Further, exports of auto-components, that is an input to market for exports of motor vehicles and the export of motor vehicles itself, embodies a large proportion of foreign value added (53% in 2011). Given the fact that the industry is a part of the value chain, the increase in exports would depend on the movements in the exchange rate of the countries to which India exports. So it is possible that the appreciation of India's exchange rate with major trading partners would lead to higher exports, since the trading partners would be able to export more.

Over the period 2000–14, the share of exports of organic chemicals went up, accompanied by declining net terms of trade (Figure 3A.4). The declining prices of chemicals have attracted anti-dumping sanctions against India. Between 1995 and 2011, of 825 anti-dumping cases at the WTO, 275 were filed against India in chemicals and allied industries.

As mentioned earlier, the rise in the share of organic chemicals and their exports was part of the shift of polluting industries to the developing countries. Over this period, India's share in exports of developing countries increased from 4 per cent to 7.5 per cent (Table A3.8). Given such a shift in production of chemicals to India, within this category the major group of export items consists of inputs to the pharmaceutical industry and polymers under the category of "other organic compounds." Organic chemicals exported by India serve as inputs to industries. Further, exports of chemicals by countries such as India have been driven by shift of production to developing countries (as shown in Figure 3.8), as is put forth by the "pollution haven hypothesis" (Francis, 2015). The shift of production to developing

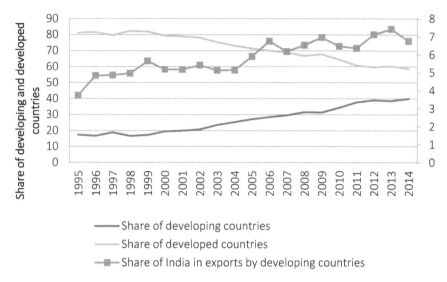

Figure 3.8 Share of world exports of organic chemicals

Source: UNCTAD

countries makes the other economies dependent on imports for the necessary inputs, which may result in an increase in exports even when the exchange rate appreciates. The imports of organic chemicals, just as with the other manufactured imports such as machinery, were observed to be inelastic.

The export and import of mineral fuels, as was discussed earlier, is the result of domestic incentives that encourage companies to import, process, and export the output. The exports in this sector have the highest import content. As per Figure 3.3, the foreign value added of exports of petroleum products was 56 per cent in 2011. Based on these facts, it is expected that the exchange rate bears little or no relationship with the trade of petroleum products. The coefficients from the regression corroborate that the exchange rate is not a determinant of the trade in this sector, as was shown for oil trade in the previous chapter.

The imports of ores (slag and ash) increased over time both in quantity and in their unit value, except for in 2013–14 and 2014–15 when unit values declined owed to a declining demand for iron ore by China. India is the world's fourth largest importer of ores, at 3.5 per cent of world imports in 2014. These imports consist of iron ore (5%), ferrous wastes (23%), copper ore (38%), and non-ferrous waste (20%). The increase observed in the imports are in part the result of the increase in imports in the years following 2011 after the ban on mining of iron ore in the states of Goa and Karnataka to curb illegal mining.[27]

The other recent trend has been the increase in cheaper imports of copper from Japan[28] that have threatened domestic units. This was the result of the FTAs signed between India and Japan that brought down the duty on refined copper.[29] A similar story emerges for the other major import category, which is non-ferrous scrap. Non-ferrous scrap was used by the domestic recycling industry; however, the inverted duty that has made the import of finished products cheaper has also rendered the business of scrap unviable.[30] India has become an important destination for these imports since the slowdown of imports to China. Therefore, imports of the various components within this category are driven by a variety of factors. Thus, from the estimated coefficient for exchange rate, it can be seen that the real exchange rate has no impact on imports, including that of inorganic chemicals.

India is among the largest exporters of iron and steel, of which pig iron and sponge iron are the top exports in this category. These two sub-categories are considered less refined and are used by heavy industries. Three factors emerge as significant for exports in this sector. First, though India is among the top exporters, it has faced stiff competition from China in exports of steel. Therefore, the increase in exports between 1999 and 2005 was reversed between 2010 and 2014. Second, exports of iron and steel have been offered DEPB benefits that allow them to import duty free imports.[31] Third, India signed a Comprehensive Economic Partnership Agreement with ASEAN (and therefore with South Korea) as well as with Japan that brought down the tariffs on imports, leading to lower capacity utilisation in the domestic industry. The estimated coefficient for exports is insignificant, reflecting the fact that other factors dominated compared to the exchange rate.

In fact, after the implementation of the CEPAs, cheaper imports dealt a severe blow to the domestic market for iron and steel.[32] Of late there have been concerns with regard to steel being dumped by China. Therefore, it is possible that the price competition from China as the CEPA treaties delivered a severe blow to domestic steel (Table 3A.20).[33] This is reflected in the inelasticity of imports.

Last, as was shown at the beginning of the section, labour intensive products respond to the exchange rate. The estimated result for apparel corroborates the results of the panel regression. The rise of exports of inputs such as cotton and yarn to apparel exporters such as China and Bangladesh has reduced the supply of inputs to domestic weavers. Along with domestic challenges to apparel production, such as lack of technology and inability to achieve scales required to compete with other apparel exporters, this has adversely affected the apparel industry. India competes with the Asian apparel exporters and, as is estimated, the REER depreciation would have a positive impact on exports.

Do exchange rates matter for exports?
A firm level analysis

Another disaggregate analysis is possible using firm level information. Other than estimating this relationship for the overall exports that have been reported in earlier sections, it is useful to ascertain if firm behaviour is at all altered by movement in exchange rate. In this section, the impact of the exchange rate on a firm's decision to exports is assessed using the panel approach. Here, the companies chosen operate in the manufacturing sector in NIC division 10–32. All companies that reported throughout or for most of the period 2000–14 were selected.

So far two studies have looked at the subject of the impact of exchange rates on firm level exports in India. Cheung and Sengupta (2013) found that firms respond asymmetrically to exchange rates, responding to the negative impact of an appreciation than to depreciation. The dependent variable that they use in their baseline case is the share of exports in total sales, which they find is negatively related to the changes in REER. As per the study, a 1 per cent appreciation of the exchange rate leads to a 6.3 per cent decline in the export as a share of sales of the firm. The study controlled for the firm level factors that may in part explain the exports of a firm. They found that even with the introduction of an interaction term for firm characteristics along with REER, the impact of the exchange rate does not attenuate. As a refinement, they used real exports (deflated by WPI and CPI) as well as NEER as a measure. They found that the results in the study do not change with the use of real value of exports as a dependent variable.

In another study, Dhasmana (2013) verified the relationship between the exchange rate and the firm output for 250 Indian manufacturing firms. The study found that "real exchange rate movements have a significant impact on Indian firms' performance through the cost as well as the revenue channel." This study too lends support to the asymmetric response to exchange rates in the scenario of the over-valued exchange rate. The study was limited to large publicly listed companies.

Taking this recent strand of literature for India, this section seeks to answer whether the exchange rate, or REER, has any impact on exports of the firm operating in the manufacturing sector. Cheung and Sengupta (2013) presented a result that is indicative of a compositional shift of production in favour of exports and, Dhasmana (2013) estimated exports for large companies and found that the exchange rate is an important determinant of exports in addition to market power and mark ups.

Taking only companies reporting export of goods, the share of exports as well as total exports are taken as measures to answer two questions: (1) what happens to exports when the exchange rate changes, and (2) do companies tend to shift production in favour of exports with a change in exchange rate?

The rise in the import intensity of production has been discussed in much detail. Building on this argument, the first explanatory variable introduced in this section is the import of raw materials and finished goods by the firm.

The main hypothesis tested in this section is whether exchange rate works as an instrument to influence firm level exports. For this purpose, the REER is taken as the independent variable in the equation. Theoretically, this may be appropriate, since the REER is shown to respond to factors such as capital flows that are independent of the trade balance. Other than the exchange rate, the market power of the firm estimated by the share of its sales in domestic sales, incentives to exports measured by the effective corporate tax rate, and imports are taken as determinants in the equation for exports.

The extent of market power may play an important role in a firm's ability to export. For example, the firm's ability to export may be enhanced by the scale of its operation. The share of sales of a company in total sales of that industry at the two-digit NIC level is taken as a measure for market power.

The export sector in India receives incentives in the form of duty drawback and tax breaks to units operating in SEZs. Each company reports the fiscal incentives that it availed during a particular year. While indirect tax incentives were reported for the companies over the years, these incentives have slowly been replaced by the predominance of tax breaks under sections 10A, 10AA, 80IA, and 80IB of the Income Tax Act. Since these are not directly measurable for the sample of companies, it is assumed that effective corporate tax rate (corporate tax by PBT) must reflect such benefit[34] and therefore has been used as a proxy. The hypothesis here is that companies availing of these tax incentives and therefore facing lower rates of tax would tend to report higher exports. In the sample of companies, on average, exporting companies have over the years reported a lower effective tax rate (27%) than those that did not report exports (30%). The lower corporate tax rate, therefore, indicates some benefits accruing to the company.[35] Taking the sample of exporters, the question being asked is whether the higher level of benefits translates into higher value of exports.

The samples of selected companies are comprised of 5,109 exporting companies operating in the manufacturing sector, and the sample period comprises the financial years from 2000 to 2014. Note that in order to ensure that the sample of companies selected for the analysis is stable, all companies that merged or stopped reporting were dropped from the sample. The companies selected for the analysis over the period accounted for approximately 50 per cent of total non-oil exports (see the Appendix, Figure 3A.1).

The following equation is estimated for exports:

$$logexports_{it} = \alpha + \beta_1 logimports_{it} + \beta_2 logreer_{it} \\ + \beta_3 CT\,by\,PBT_{it} + \beta_3\,Share\,of\,sales\,in\,industry_{it} \tag{3.3}$$

The exports are predicted using a system GMM.[36] Using the specification tests, the fixed effects model[37] is chosen. The estimated models are reported in Table 3.7.

Table 3.7 GMM estimates for firm level exports for manufacturing sector

Independent variables	Coefficient	Standard error	t-stat	P value
Dependent variable: log (exports) GMM estimates				
Log (imports)	0.65	0.04	14.51	0
Log (REER)	−0.19	0.11	−1.67	0.094
CT by PBT	−0.24	0.17	−1.41	0.16
Share of sales	−0.16	0.04	−3.68	0
constant	0.55	0.51	1.07	0.283
R square	0.71			

From Table 3.7 it can be seen that exchange rate depreciation leads to higher value of exports. Though the coefficient for REER in the specification is significant only at the 10 per cent level, it can be said that exchange rate depreciation translates into higher value of manufacturing exports both in the share of the sales of the firm and in total value.

The other important question of whether corporate tax incentives have had any impact on the firm's ability to export more finds very little support. The results for the effective corporate tax is insignificant, indicating that there is neither a composition nor a value shift in favour of exports owing to incentives, even though on average, the tax rate has been lower for exporting firms.

The argument of the rise in import intensity has been put forth earlier for the overall exports by India, and a similar trend has been observed for the major items of exports. Keeping the results in mind, imports were introduced in equation 3.3. The estimated coefficient is positive and significant, thus indicating that higher exports are associated with higher imports. Therefore, a firm's ability to export is positively associated with its capacity to import. As for the market power of the company, companies with a higher share of industry sales export less than those with smaller shares.

To conclude, firm level estimates corroborate the overall results that exchange rate depreciation (appreciation) leads to higher (lower) value of exports by companies. The results described here are after controlling for the effects of imports on exports and that of exchange rate on the former. Therefore, even though imports are associated with higher exports, appreciation tends to lower exports.

Conclusion

The period 2000–14 was marked by a change in the product composition of exports, as commodities such as petroleum and cotton emerged among the top exports and the shares of commodities such as apparel declined. The structure of imports, however, remained largely unchanged. This shift cannot be viewed positively, especially since it has been accompanied by trade deficits within categories of goods that constitute a major share of exports. For example, machinery, gems and jewellery, organic chemicals, and iron and steel were in deficit in 2014. The increase in exports during this period was accompanied by a greater increase in imports. Firm level evidence for manufacturing, in fact, supports the hypothesis of rising import dependence of exports. Some of these imports are, in fact, for export purposes. There is also evidence to suggest that India now exports commodities such as cotton, in which it is possesses RCA. However, this was accompanied by a reduction in share of apparel exports. In terms of trade balances of major commodities, there has been a substantial expansion in the trade deficit for oil.

One important result that emerges from this analysis is that though the basket of exported goods is not similar for India and China, in terms of the major commodities of exports, India faces stiff competition from China. Some of India's traditional exports, such as leather and apparel, were severely affected by the growth in exports from China. The other important point is that India has been able to retain or gain RCA in some commodities, i.e. cotton, meat, and rice, as a result of both global factors and India's ability to cut prices.

Further, India has exported its major commodities to many countries, whereas for imports it has relied on a few countries. India exported to many countries, the USA being the largest destination, followed by African countries and developing Asia in 2014. For imports, China emerged as the dominant trading partner.

Last, the evidence on exchange rate's impact on exports supports the argument that depreciation will lead to higher exports by firms operating in the manufacturing sector and, within manufacturing, commodities such as pharmaceutical, machinery, apparel, and gems and jewellery respond as expected. For some categories, such as organic chemicals and vehicles, the exchange rate does not affect trade. The type of product and the firms undertaking such production determine whether the exchange rate has an impact on exports. However, for imports, inelasticity of demand is observed for most commodities. This is in line with the rise in import intensity of production observed for various sectors within manufacturing. The firm level analysis corroborates the results observed in the commodity-wise analysis. Therefore, it can be said that exports of manufacturing products such as machinery, pharmaceuticals, gems and jewellery, and textiles are sensitive to changes in the exchange rate. The impact for the labour intensive products is more pronounced when taken separately.[38]

Other than the exchange rate, from the firm level analysis, a tendency emerges for firms with smaller market shares to export more. The lower effective corporate tax rates that incorporate the impact of incentives seem to have no significant impact on exports.

Factors other than the exchange rate seem to drive exports. Similarly, the tariff structure on imports exerts a significant influence on the level of imports. Therefore, while the exchange rate with the major destinations does have significant influence, other factors simultaneously influence trade.

Appendix

Table 3A.1 Exports of gems and jewellery

Country	2000–01		2014–15	
	Value (US$ million)	Share (%)	Value (US$ million)	Share (%)
USA	2,742	36.9	8,420	20.3
Hong Kong	1,745	23.5	12,206	29.4
Belgium	909	12.2	2,680	6.5
UAE	444	6.0	12,280	29.6
Japan	386	5.2	283	0.7
Israel	274	3.7	1,183	2.8
Thailand	191	2.6	665	1.6
UK	149	2.0	509	1.2
Switzerland	143	1.9	294	0.7
Singapore	122	1.6	493	1.2
Germany	78	1.0	114	0.3
Italy	34	0.5	132	0.3
Australia	29	0.4	288	0.7
Total	7,246	97.6	39,547	95.2

Source: DGCIS

Table 3A.2 Exports of cereals

Country	2000–01		2014–15	
	Value (US$ million)	Share (%)	Value (US$ million)	Share (%)
Saudi Arabia	287	39	1,300	14
Iran	–	–	1,240	13
Bangladesh	93	13	852	9
UAE	39	5	581	6

Country	2000–01		2014–15	
	Value (US$ million)	Share (%)	Value (US$ million)	Share (%)
Indonesia	1	0	336	4
Sri Lanka	1	0	327	3
Nepal	5	1	298	3
Yemen	13	2	286	3
Iraq	5	1	285	3
Kuwait	52	7	272	3
Benin	–	–	251	3
Qatar	2	0	236	2
Senegal	–	–	227	2
Turkey	0	0	186	2
Oman	13	2	173	2
UK	67	9	160	2
USA	30	4	159	2
Malaysia	5	1	154	2
Guinea	0	0	153	2
South Africa	15	2	147	2
Nigeria	0	0	132	1
Singapore	9	1	109	1
Vietnam	2	0	108	1
Total	640	86	7,971	83

Source: DGCIS

Table 3A.3 Exports of cotton

Country	2000–01		2014–15	
	Value (US$ million)	Share (%)	Value (US$ million)	Share (%)
China	70	3	2,278	30
Bangladesh	215	9	1,524	20
Vietnam	7	0	437	6
Sri Lanka	69	3	226	3
Korea	129	5	224	3
Egypt	50	2	216	3
Pakistan	0	0	200	3
UAE	91	4	143	2
Peru	1	0	130	2
Portugal	25	1	125	2
Italy	118	5	116	2

(Continued)

Table 3A.3 (Continued)

Country	2000–01		2014–15	
	Value (US$ million)	Share (%)	Value (US$ million)	Share (%)
Colombia	16	1	106	1
Togo	20	1	96	1
Turkey	32	1	95	1
Indonesia	21	1	93	1
Hong Kong	205	8	92	1
USA	119	5	91	1
Total	1,187	49	6,191	80

Source: DGCIS

Table 3A.4 Exports of non-electrical machinery

Country	2000–01		2014–15	
	Value (US$ million)	Share (%)	Value (US$ million)	Share (%)
USA	230	16	2,157	16
UK	103	7	745	5
UAE	66	5	711	5
Germany	96	7	600	4
China	18	1	500	4
Singapore	46	3	426	3
Turkey	14	1	402	3
Italy	34	2	384	3
Saudi Arabia	20	1	379	3
Nigeria	56	4	367	3
Bangladesh	60	4	352	3
Russia	8	1	323	2
Indonesia	15	1	322	2
Malaysia	145	10	319	2
France	20	1	290	2
Thailand	15	1	274	2
Nepal	10	1	242	2
Japan	19	1	229	2
Brazil	11	1	226	2
Iran	10	1	212	2
South Africa	16	1	192	1
Vietnam	18	1	175	1
Total	1,028	72	9,828	71

Source: DGCIS

Table 3A.5 Exports of electrical machinery

Country	2000–01		2014–15	
	Value (US$ million)	Share (%)	Value (US$ million)	Share (%)
USA	212	16	1,267	15
UAE	64	5	616	7
Germany	57	4	438	5
UK	82	6	418	5
Netherlands	37	3	319	4
China	14	1	280	3
France	30	2	274	3
Saudi Arabia	17	1	251	3
Singapore	115	9	226	3
Hong Kong	161	12	219	3
Nigeria	25	2	165	2
Israel	5	0	163	2
Iran	18	1	162	2
Malaysia	28	2	159	2
Bangladesh	19	1	150	2
Indonesia	9	1	149	2
Sri Lanka	22	2	138	2
Vietnam	2	0	137	2
Japan	24	2	126	1
Myanmar	3	0	125	1
Nepal	5	0	122	1
Oman	9	1	112	1
Turkey	5	0	109	1
Total	963	75	6,123	70

Source: DGCIS

Table 3A.6 Exports of vehicles

Country	2000–01		2014–15	
	Value (US$ million)	Share (%)	Value (US$ million)	Share (%)
USA	120	13	1,288	9
Mexico	26	3	1,027	7
South Africa	15	2	878	6
Sri Lanka	79	8	668	5
Turkey	25	3	603	4
Bangladesh	61	7	571	4

(Continued)

Table 3A.6 (Continued)

| Country | 2000–01 | | 2014–15 | |
	Value (US$ million)	Share (%)	Value (US$ million)	Share (%)
UK	57	6	553	4
Nigeria	39	4	501	3
UAE	22	2	445	3
Colombia	5	1	438	3
Nepal	15	2	417	3
Algeria	4	0	414	3
Italy	53	6	396	3
Egypt	14	2	343	2
Germany	35	4	300	2
Thailand	5	1	246	2
Indonesia	23	3	240	2
Brazil	8	1	235	2
Saudi Arabia	6	1	229	2
Philippines	3	0	224	2
Australia	8	1	205	1
Netherlands	22	2	194	1
Spain	21	2	170	1
Total	667	72	10,583	73

Source: DGCIS

Table 3A.7 Exports of pharmaceuticals

| Country | 2000–01 | | 2014–15 | |
	Value (US$ million)	Share (%)	Value (US$ million)	Share (%)
USA	56	6	3,769	33
South Africa	13	1	458	4
UK	23	2	440	4
Russia	100	11	411	4
Nigeria	74	8	382	3
Kenya	14	1	253	2
Brazil	19	2	224	2
Tanzania	11	1	193	2
Australia	8	1	180	2
Ghana	10	1	173	1
Germany	37	4	169	1
Myanmar	11	1	169	1

Country	2000–01		2014–15	
	Value (US$ million)	Share (%)	Value (US$ million)	Share (%)
Netherlands	24	3	168	1
Vietnam	34	4	165	1
Sri Lanka	34	4	158	1
Uganda	10	1	154	1
Nepal	28	3	145	1
Venezuela	2	0	144	1
France	8	1	143	1
Canada	8	1	136	1
Philippines	8	1	135	1
Ethiopia	4	0	113	1
Malawi	1	0	109	1
Total	535	57	8,390	72

Source: DGCIS

Table 3A.8 Exports of organic chemicals

Country	2000–01		2014–15	
	Value (US$ million)	Share (%)	Value (US$ million)	Share (%)
USA	222	13	1,638	14
China	108	6	1,045	9
Germany	113	7	598	5
Indonesia	36	2	537	5
Malaysia	15	1	437	4
Belgium	28	2	426	4
Spain	55	3	394	3
Netherlands	55	3	393	3
Brazil	77	4	362	3
Japan	44	3	344	3
Italy	63	4	299	3
Korea	35	2	279	2
Singapore	47	3	277	2
Saudi Arabia	17	1	270	2
UAE	34	2	262	2
Switzerland	39	2	252	2
UK	62	4	244	2

(Continued)

Table 3A.8 (Continued)

Country	2000–01		2014–15	
	Value (US$ million)	Share (%)	Value (US$ million)	Share (%)
Mexico	29	2	244	2
Iran	27	2	240	2
Turkey	22	1	235	2
Pakistan	36	2	225	2
Thailand	54	3	200	2
Israel	24	1	186	2
Total	1,243	72	9,387	79

Source: DGCIS

Table 3A.9 Export of apparel

Country	2000–01		2014–15	
	Value (US$ million)	Share (%)	Value (US$ million)	Share (%)
USA	1,376	36	1,995	22
UAE	422	11	1,508	16
UK	271	7	956	10
Germany	222	6	575	6
Spain	58	2	437	5
France	224	6	415	5
Netherlands	90	2	230	2
Italy	103	3	194	2
Denmark	34	1	192	2
Saudi Arabia	85	2	172	2
Japan	99	3	169	2
Brazil	8	0	150	2
Malaysia	21	1	146	2
Canada	114	3	133	1
Belgium	47	1	110	1
Sweden	23	1	98	1

Source: DGCIS

Table 3A.10 Exports of mineral fuels

Country	2000–01		2014–15	
	Value (US$ million)	Share (%)	Value (US$ million)	Share (%)
UAE	31	2	6,520	11
Saudi Arabia	0	0	5,570	10
Singapore	0	0	5,333	9
USA	2	0	3,885	7
Brazil	1	0	3,155	5
Unspecified	–	–	2,854	5
Kenya	0	0	2,734	5
Netherlands	1	0	2,472	4
Japan	8	0	1,853	3
Mozambique	–	–	1,646	3
South Africa	0	0	1,581	3
Mauritius	0	0	1,546	3
Korea	5	0	1,532	3
Tanzania	1	0	1,436	2
Turkey	2	0	1,363	2
Nepal	6	0	1,303	2
China	1	0	1,291	2
Malaysia	1	0	1,246	2
Israel	–	–	1,049	2
Total	60	3	48,369	84

Source: DGCIS

Table 3A.11 Imports of gems and jewellery

Country	2000–01		2014–15	
	Value (US$ million)	Share (%)	Value (US$ million)	Share (%)
Switzerland	2,824	29.1	20,385	32.7
Belgium	2,575	26.5	9,017	14.5
UAE	249	2.6	8,795	14.1
Hong Kong	493	5.1	4,095	6.6
USA	173	1.8	3,522	5.6
South Africa	603	6.2	1,896	3.0
Australia	23	0.2	1,647	2.6
Russia	20	0.2	1,273	2.0
China	27	0.3	1,231	2.0

(Continued)

Table 3A.11 (Continued)

Country	2000–01		2014–15	
	Value (US$ million)	Share (%)	Value (US$ million)	Share (%)
UK	2,204	22.7	1,152	1.8
Israel	300	3.1	1,091	1.7
Ghana	5	0.0	1,048	1.7
Botswana	–	–	926	1.5
Saudi Arabia	5	0.1	759	1.2
Tanzania	13	0.1	603	1.0
Canada	6	0.1	581	0.9
Germany	10	0.1	458	0.7
Korea	5	0.1	374	0.6
Total	9,535	98	58,853	94

Source: DGCIS

Table 3A.12 Imports of ores, slag, and ash

Country	2000–01		2014–15	
	Value (US$ million)	Share (%)	Value (US$ million)	Share (%)
Chile	50	17	2,615	35.5
Australia	90	31	1,146	15.6
South Africa	4	1	852	11.6
Brazil	0	0	540	7.3
Indonesia	20	7	512	6.9
Canada	8	3	308	4.2
Peru	4	1	264	3.6
Eritrea	–	–	223	3.0
Guinea	–	–	105	1.4
Botswana	–	–	86	1.2
Lao	–	–	67	0.9
Gabon	0	0	54	0.7
China	17	6	50	0.7
Argentina	26	9	47	0.6
Turkey	1	0	46	0.6
China	17	6	50	1
Bahrain	11	4	0	0
Jordan	11	4	0	0
Canada	8	3	308	4

Country	2000–01		2014–15	
	Value (US$ million)	Share (%)	Value (US$ million)	Share (%)
Colombia	6	2	0	0
Mexico	6	2	17	0
USA	6	2	28	0
Iran	5	2	1	0
Peru	4	1	264	4
Total	235	82	7,074	96

Source: DGCIS

Table 3A.13 Imports of organic chemicals

Country	2000–01		2014–15	
	Value (US$ million)	Share (%)	Value (US$ million)	Share (%)
China	249	16	6,328	35.7
Singapore	113	7	1,428	8.0
Saudi Arabia	131	8	1,265	7.1
Korea	51	3	943	5.3
Kuwait	5	0	833	4.7
USA	180	11	750	4.2
Germany	117	7	726	4.1
Iran	36	2	638	3.6
Taiwan	23	1	553	3.1
Malaysia	45	3	520	2.9
Thailand	9	1	496	2.8
Japan	122	8	413	2.3
Qatar	18	1	256	1.4
Oman	0	0	237	1.3
Indonesia	51	3	229	1.3
Italy	43	3	224	1.3
France	46	3	209	1.2
Netherlands	68	4	202	1
Switzerland	44	3	185	1
Spain	34	2	165	1
Belgium	26	2	143	1
Total	1,307	82	16,250	92

Source: DGCIS

Table 3A.14 Imports of inorganic chemicals

Country	2000–01		2014–15	
	Value (US$ million)	Share (%)	Value (US$ million)	Share (%)
China	51	5	738	14
Morocco	277	25	706	14
Iran	22	2	430	8
USA	51	5	373	7
Saudi Arabia	115	11	296	6
Qatar	39	4	259	5
Australia	2	0	256	5
Ukraine	1	0	211	4
Tunisia	82	8	173	3
Korea	9	1	146	3
Germany	21	2	146	3
Jordan	34	3	130	3
Vietnam	–	–	117	2
Senegal	16	1	114	2
Chile	2	0	82	2
Japan	20	2	79	2
Russia	11	1	68	1
Malaysia	3	0	59	1
Turkey	5	0	58	1
Total	760	70	4,441	86

Source: DGCIS

Table 3A.15 Imports of fertilisers

Country	2000–01		2014–15	
	Value (US$ million)	Share (%)	Value (US$ million)	Share (%)
China	132	8.1	3,155	49.4
Saudi Arabia			613	9.6
Russia	0	0	457	7.2
Canada	14	0.8	371	5.8
USA	301	18.5	304	4.8
Jordan	0	0	281	4.4
Oman	0	0	267	4.2
Iran	0	0	230	3.6
Israel	7	0.4	222	3.5

Country	2000–01		2014–15	
	Value (US$ million)	Share (%)	Value (US$ million)	Share (%)
Belarus	0		146	2.3
Lithuania	0	0	88	1.4
Germany	235	14.4	75	1.2
Indonesia	117	7.2	43	0.7
UAE	0	0.00	23	0.4
Norway	3	0.1	16	0.3
Switzerland	130.45	8.0		
France	103.14	6.3		
Italy	89.72	5.5		
Brazil	66.69	4.1		
Denmark	58.71	3.6		
Belgium	48.96	3.0		

Source: DGCIS

Table 3A.16 Imports of non-electrical machinery

Country	2000–01		2014–15	
	Value (US$ million)	Share (%)	Value (US$ million)	Share (%)
China	189	4	10,144.22	31.9
Germany	534	13	3,575.92	11.3
USA	615	15	3,010.04	9.5
Japan	481	11	2,466.5	7.8
Korea	164	4	1,706.39	5.4
Italy	239	6	1,512.63	4.7
Thailand	122	3	1,382.71	4.3
Singapore	475	11	1,093.45	3.4
Malaysia	251	6	709.07	2.2
UK	193	5	699.33	2.2
Taiwan	164	4	600.63	1.9
France	107	3	511.94	1.6
Switzerland	93	2	401.1	1.3
Belgium	55	1	298.33	0.9
Netherlands	43	1	291.95	0.9
Spain	19	0	260.67	0.8
Total	3,744	88	28,665	90

Source: DGCIS

Table 3A.17 Imports of electrical machinery

Country	2000–01		2014–15	
	Value (US$ million)	Share (%)	Value (US$ million)	Share (%)
China	161	6	16,738	50.5
Korea	149	6	2,460	7.4
USA	459	17	1,713	5.2
Germany	222	8	1,407	4.2
Malaysia	107	4	1,247	3.8
Vietnam	1	0	1,239	3.7
Japan	220	8	960	2.9
Singapore	347	13	907	2.7
Taiwan	102	4	804	2.4
Thailand	40	2	710	2.1
Hong Kong	95	4	665	2.0
Finland	50	2	447	1.3
Israel	35	1	403	1.2
France	98	4	400	1.2
Sweden	97	4	326	1.0
Total	2,183	82	30,428	92

Source: DGCIS

Table 3A.18 Imports of mineral fuels

Country	2000–01		2014–15	
	Value (US$ million)	Share (%)	Value (US$ million)	Share (%)
Saudi Arabia	267.06	1.52	23,212.9	14.8
Iraq	6.9	0.04	14,177.2	9.06
Nigeria	–	–	13,532.4	8.6
UAE	161.93	0.92	13,509	8.6
Qatar	–	–	13,415	8.6
Kuwait	48.03	0.27	12,228.7	7.8
Venezuela	–	–	11,669	7.5
Indonesia	85.58	0.48	7,497.3	4.8
Iran	30.57	0.17	7,292.1	4.7
Australia	605.75	3.45	5,720.6	3.7
Angola			4,418.3	2.8
Malaysia	10.1	0.06	2,762.7	1.8
Mexico			2,684.3	1.7

Country	2000–01		2014–15	
	Value (US$ million)	Share (%)	Value (US$ million)	Share (%)
Brazil			2,534.5	1.6
South Africa	132.51	0.75	2,512.7	1.6
Colombia			1,776.5	1.1
Unspecified countries	14,763.65	84.1	250.7	0.16
Petroleum producing countries	886.46	5.05		

Source: DGCIS

Table 3A.19 Imports of iron and steel

Country	2000–01		2014–15	
	Value (US$ million)	Share (%)	Value (US$ million)	Share (%)
China	10	1.0	20,385	32.7
Korea	66	6.9	9,017	14.5
Japan	99	10.3	8,795	14.1
UAE	32	3.4	4,095	6.6
South Africa	45	4.7	3,522	5.6
UK	96	10.1	1,896	3.0
USA	61	6.4	1,647	2.6
Germany	68	7.1	1,273	2.0
Russia	108	11.3	1,231	2.0
Malaysia	5	0.5	1,152	1.8
Singapore	24	2.5	1,091	1.7
France	19	1.9	1,048	1.7
Brazil	13	1.4	926	1.5
Ukraine	66	6.9	759	1.2
Netherlands	15	1.6	603	1.0
Taiwan	5	0.6	581	0.9
Belgium	29	3.1	458	0.7
Thailand	12	1.3	374	0.6
Australia	–	–	148.2	1.2
Sweden	–	–	142.0	1.2
Total	773	81	58,853	94

Source: DGCIS

Table 3A.20 Regression of real exchange rate and exports of iron and steel

	Exports of iron and steel
World GDP	1.23[***]
RER	0.66[**]
Dummy* RER	0.69[**]
Constant	−9.55[***]
R square	0.95

Note: * means significant at 10%, ** means significant at 5%, and *** means significant at 1%

Source: Estimated

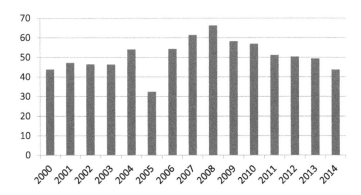

■ Share of exports reported by companies in non-oil exports of India

Figure 3A.1 Exports of companies

Source: Estimated using CMIE data

Table 3A.21 Estimated equation for gold imports

Variable	Coefficient
Log REER	−0.13 (0.21)
Log GDP	0.72[***] (0.06)
Constant	−0.98[**] (0.35)
R square	0.95

Note: * means significant at 10%, ** means significant at 5%, and *** means significant at 1%

Source: Estimated

Table 3A.22 Estimated equation for exports

Exports	Cereals	Mineral oils	Organic chemicals	Pharmaceuticals	Cotton	Articles of apparel not knitted	Gems and jewellery	Iron and steel	Non-electrical machinery	Electrical machinery	Vehicles
Log(World GDP)	0.12**	0.036***	0.96***	1.06***	0.73***	0.65***	-0.74***	1***	1.08***	1.23***	1.31***
	(0.05)	(0.067)	(0.05)	(0.04)	(0.19)	(0.04)	(0.17)	(0.104)	(0.02)	(0.06)	(0.04)
RER	0.94***	1.77	0.199***	-0.51***	0.04	-0.47*	-0.73***	0.24	-0.157***	-0.26**	0.16**
	(0.09)	(0.08)	(0.05)		(0.39)	(0.97)	(0.05)	(0.15)	(0.069)	(0.1)	(0.09)
Constant	-6.7***	-15***	-6.65***	-9***	-4.26	-5.27***	-5.94***	-7.1***	-8.48***	-10.1***	-10.4***
	(1.08)	(0.98)	(0.25)	(0.3)	(2.47)	(1.14)	(0.34)	(1.09)	(0.35)	(0.75)	(0.5)
R square	0.9	0.98	0.99	0.99		0.97	0.98	0.91	0.99	0.97	0.99

Note: * means significant at 10%, ** means significant at 5%, and *** means significant at 1%

Table 3A.23 Estimated equation for imports

Imports	Ores, slag, and ash	Mineral oils	Inorganic chemicals	Organic chemicals	Fertilisers	Gems and jewellery	Iron and steel	Non-electrical machinery	Electrical machinery	Vehicles
Log(India GDP)	2.24***	1.9***	1.31***	1.62***	1.9***	1.4***	2.04***	1.67***	1.85***	0.54
	(0.13)	(0.22)		(0.05)	(0.15)	(0.11)	(0.21)	(0.09)	(0.17)	(0.63)
RER	0.02	−0.04	−0.04	−0.09**	−0.5***	0.22	−0.57*	−0.69**	−0.15	0.05
	(0.2)	(0.29)	(0.09)	(0.05)	(0.06)	(0.28)	(0.29)	(0.26)	(0.09)	(0.11)
Constant	−7.95***	−1.86	0.124	−2.5***	−6.5***	0.2	−5.65***	−1.75**	−4.1***	−6.23***
	(1.22)	(1.02)	(0.57)	(0.35)	(1.07)	(1.4)	(1.3)	(0.64)	(0.6)	(0.6)
R square	0.91	0.98	0.94	0.99	0.89	0.95	0.92	0.96	0.94	0.98

Note: * means significant at 10%, ** means significant at 5%, and *** means significant at 1%

Prices and quantity indices for commodities

For most commodities, it can be observed that the relative prices and quantities of exports tend to move in the opposite direction. Here, the changes in the terms of trade are presented for each of the commodities with reasons for the changes.

Since the export of cereal primarily consists of rice, and it is of interest whether the quantity or the price played an important role in determining how much India exported of this commodity, we take the unit value of exports and the quantities. As discussed earlier, the export of non-basmati rice was banned in 2007–08. Figure 3A.2 shows that there had been a decline in the quantity of exports following this ban. Meanwhile, the rise in the global prices is reflected in the rise in price (or unit value) of rice exports. In 2011, when the government lifted the ban and put the stocks in the market along with the reduction of MEP, the unit value declined while the quantity exported expanded. Therefore, the changes in unit value and quantity reflect the changes in policy.

The other primary commodity in which India is a dominant exporter is cotton. From Figure 3A.5, it is evident that the period 2000–13 was one of stable export prices of cotton accompanied by a rise in the quantum of cotton exports. The increase in quantum of exports, therefore, resulted in an increase in the overall value of exports. In 2013, cotton exports accounted for 21.3 per cent of world exports and 1.4 per cent of India's exports.

The net terms of trade (Px/Pm) for gems and jewellery declined over the period 2000–14, whereas the quantity of exports expanded faster than that of imports (Figure 3A.11). However, this increase in quantity of exports did not result in an improvement in the trade deficit. Figures 3.1 and 3.2 show that the trade deficit for gems and jewellery expanded over the period of analysis. Such an expansion is, in fact, expected, since the quantities of imports surpass those of imports and declining prices of exports only worsen the deficit.

On the other hand, the net terms of trade for the mineral fuels have been volatile and increasing. However, the quantum of imports has expanded much faster than those of export (Figure 3A.3). Therefore, the rise in price of exports along with a significant expansion of quantity of imports has resulted in a significant expansion of the trade deficit. Thus the two sectors – gems and jewellery, and mineral fuels – that contribute a large share to exports and are also major items of imports have seen increases in trade deficits. Such an increase has resulted from the quantum of imports that have exceeded that of exports in value and also in terms of rate of growth for minerals.

With respect to organic chemicals, India saw a massive increase in the quantum of exports until 2006–07, after which they declined; whereas the prices have been steady between 2000 and 2014. The decline in the quantum of exports was accompanied by a rise in the trade deficit after 2006. Within the category of organic chemicals, synthetic dyes are among the few commodities for which India is revealed to have a comparative advantage; nevertheless, the overall deficit for organic chemicals increased over time.

In the category of machinery, electrical and non-electrical, as well as vehicles and parts thereof, India witnessed a sharp increase in the relative price of exports, whereas the relative quantities declined (Figures 3A.8, 3A.9, and 3A.10). The increase in foreign value added in this segment (as shown in Figure 3.3) reflects on the relative importance of imports. Though the terms of trade were favourable over the period, it can be said that any reversal in this trend is expected to have an adverse impact on the balance of trade. In fact, in Figures 3.1 and 3.2, it was shown that for machinery the gains in the share of exports were accompanied by a rise in the deficit for this sector between 2000 and 2014.

The unit price of apparel exports remained stable over time; however, the unit price of imports declined (Figures 3A.12 and 3A.13). This has resulted in the increase in the net terms of trade. The quantities, on the other hand, increased for exports, but the recent expansion in the apparel imports lowered the Qx/Qm ratio. In absolute terms, India still remains a net exporter of apparel. However, such trends are worrying. The domestic industry for apparel could suffer since it must compete to procure cotton, which is shipped to apparel exporters, accompanied by an expansion in imports of apparel. The unit value of imports of fertilisers as well as their quantity increased over the decade until 2008, after which there was a reversal in unit value and, in 2011, in the quantity. The increase in the demand for fertilisers, in spite of rising prices, resulted from the shortfall in the domestic production of fertilisers.

In the case of pharmaceuticals, the expansion of pharmaceutical exports was accompanied by an increase in unit value as well as quantum of exports (Figure 3A.14). The growing presence of foreign pharmaceutical companies in the Indian market, which has been a feature post 2005 along with massive expansion in exports to the USA, was also accompanied by an increase in prices. While the share of African countries remained the same over the period, the share of developing Asia declined. Thus, the increase in prices was accompanied by an expansion of sales to the developed countries.

The quantum of iron and steel exports expanded more slowly than the imports (Figure 3A.7). This was the result of relatively cheaper supply of steel by China as well as the lower duty on imports from South Korea and Japan. This, coupled with stable terms of trade, resulted in a trade deficit for iron and steel.

Lastly, the imports of ores comprise copper ores for which India is heavily import-dependent,[39] other than for Hindustan copper that sources the ore from its captive mines. There was an expansion in cheaper imports from ASEAN countries, which was a cause of concern for domestic producers of copper.[40] This, in fact, resulted in the switch of the sector from one with a surplus to one with a deficit. Indeed, imports of scrap for the purpose of recycling also increased (Figure 3A.16).

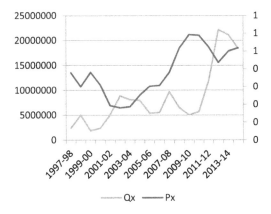

Figure 3A.2 Terms of trade for cereals

Source: Figures 3A.2 to 3A.16 are constructed from DGCIS data.

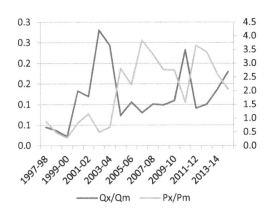

Figure 3A.3 Terms of trade for minerals and fuels

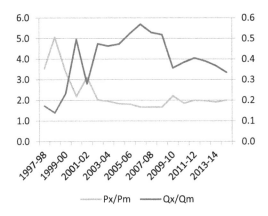

Figure 3A.4 Terms of trade for organic chemicals

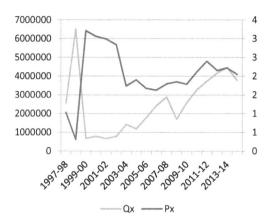

Figure 3A.5 Terms of trade for cotton

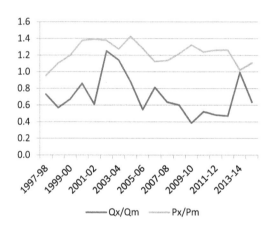

Figure 3A.6 Terms of trade for iron and steel

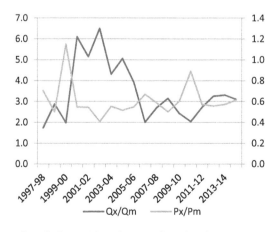

Figure 3A.7 Terms of trade for articles of iron and steel

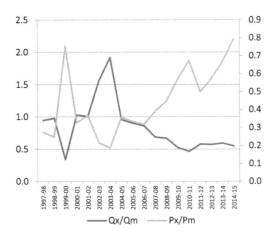

Figure 3A.8 Terms of trade for machinery (non-electrical)

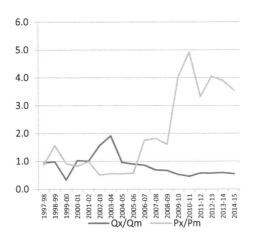

Figure 3A.9 Terms of trade for electrical machinery

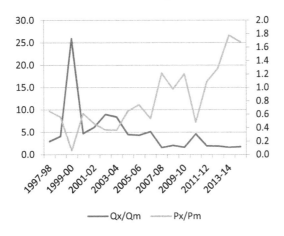

Figure 3A.10 Terms of trade for vehicles

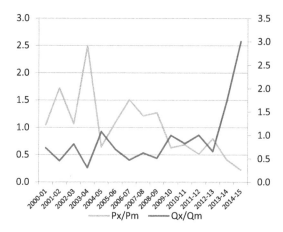

Figure 3A.11 Terms of trade for gems and jewellery

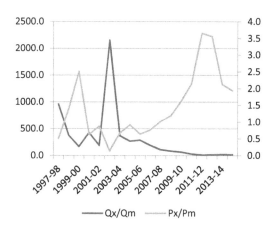

Figure 3A.12 Terms of trade for articles of apparel knitted

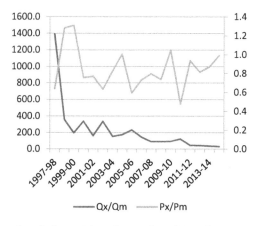

Figure 3A.13 Terms of trade for articles of apparel not knitted

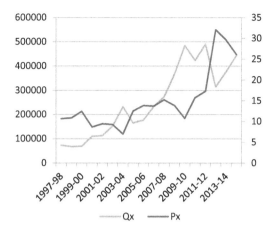

Figure 3A.14 Terms of trade for pharmaceuticals

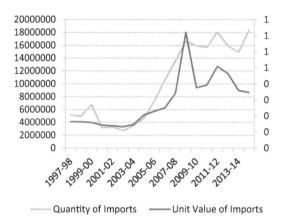

Figure 3A.15 Terms of trade for fertilisers

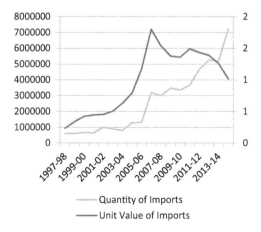

Figure 3A.16 Terms of trade for ores, slag, and ash

Notes

1 For the purpose of analysis, the two-digit HS code classification is used in this chapter.
2 "Rajiv Kumar and Amitendu Palit: Has the fuel run out of India's exports?" February 2007.
3 "End of textile quota regime – India must still spin faster to stay in place," September 2004.
4 "India wants EU to do away with import duty on its textiles," February 2016.
5 "Export cheer from engineering goods," October 2014.
6 The gems and jewellery sector is known to show a low-value addition in India (see "Jewellery export might hit 4-year high in FY16," April 2015).
7 Note that the preceding and succeeding sections entail a discussion based on the two-digit HS classification. However, to compare the product composition with the world, the tables prepared by the UNCTAD based on this classification are used.
8 "Problems & Prospects of Rice Export from India," 2007.
9 "Rice Sales from India to Reach Record as Iran Boosts Reserves," February 2014.
10 "Pakistan's basmati export hopes fade; Indian prices fall," January 2016.
11 The anti-beef movement has dealt a severe blow to the exports of two industries, viz. leather manufacturing and meat.
12 OECD-FAO Agricultural Outlook (2014: 184).
13 "Booming Chemical Production in Developing Countries Is Killing the World's Poor," September 2012.
14 "Environment and health in developing countries" (WHO).
15 Productivity & Competitiveness of Indian Manufacturing – Leather & Leather Products Sector (2010), page 12.
16 Productivity & Competitiveness of Indian Manufacturing – Leather & Leather Products Sector (2010), Page 18.
17 "India's leather exports to take a hiding," 2014.
18 "Indian diamond cutting and polishing sector," 2015.
19 Boring (2012).
20 Note that the factor intensity is identified using earlier studies.
21 The real effective exchange rate based on all currencies did not turn up significant in all cases which is in line with the overall results reported in Chapter 2.
22 The data had been corrected for heteroskedasticity and autocorrelation.
23 Note that a separate regression for the rupee value was undertaken, and it was found that REER was insignificant.
24 Government of India (DSIR).
25 The RER constructed for gold is negative (implying inelasticity) but turns up insignificant.
26 For instance, the customs duty on seamless tubes of alloy/non-alloy steels that find usage in boilers and heat exchangers is 10 per cent, while the customs duty on boilers and heat exchangers is 7.5 per cent. Also, zero duty EPCG scheme allows import of capital goods (including CKD/SKD – completely-knocked-down/semi-knocked-down – as well as computer software systems) for pre-production, production, and post-production at zero customs duty (EXIM, 2014).
27 "India iron ore imports hit record 6.8 million tonnes as prices fall," December 2014.
28 "The India-Japan comprehensive economic partnership agreement or CEPA has led to copper cathode imports from the partner rising by over 20 times

between 2013–14 and 2014–15, according to industry submissions to the government."
29 "As cheaper imports increases copper industry sends SOS to government," October 2014.
30 "Dumping of cheaper finished products cuts into scrap imports," October 2015.
31 "Iron, steel exports plunge 41% to $4.57 billion in September," October 2015.
32 "Steel makers approach government to look into dumping by foreign players," April 2015.
33 Also, only in the case of exports of iron and steel is the dummy significant.
34 Unless the company is mired in tax litigation.
35 While other tax practices may yield lower effective rates, the presumption here is that the main cause for lower rates will be the fiscal benefits.
36 Since imports are also endogenously determined. For this purpose, REER is used as an instrument.
37 Even if one selects the random effects model, the results do not change.
38 The price-quantity adjustments discussed in detail in appendix explain these results. For detailed discussion see Appendix.
39 " Smelting Key to India's copper Industry," October 2008
40 "As cheaper imports increases copper industry sends SOS to Government," 2015.

References

"As cheaper imports increases copper industry sends SOS to government," October 2014 available at http://economictimes.indiatimes.com/articleshow/49344924.cms?utm_source=contentofinterest&utm_medium=text&utm_campaign=cppst

Bain, 2015. "The global diamond industry", available at www.bain.com/Images/FINAL%20bain_diamond_report_2015_01122015.pdf

Balassa, B., 1965. Trade liberalisation and "revealed" comparative advantage 1. *The Manchester School, 33*(2), pp. 99–123.

Batra, A., and Khan, Z., 2005. Revealed comparative advantage: An analysis for India and China. Working Paper No. 168.

"Booming chemical production in developing countries is killing the world's poor," September 2012 available at http://motherboard.vice.com/blog/booming-chemical-production-in-developing-countries-is-killing-the-world-s-poor

Boring, A., 2012. Offshoring Production and Intra-Industry Trade. ETSG 2012 Conference, Leuven.

Burange, L.G. and Chadha, S.J., 2008. India's revealed comparative advantage in merchandise trade. Mumbai University Working Paper UDE28/6/2008.

Burange, L.G. and Chaddha, S.J., 2008. India's revealed comparative advantage in merchandise trade. *Artha Vijnana, 50*(4), pp. 332–363, available at http://archive.mu.ac.in/arts/social_science/eco/pdfs/depart/dwp51.pdf

———— Textiles and garments: Export Price comparison, DSIR, available at http://www.dsir.gov.in/reports/isr1/Textiles%20and%20Garments/2_8.pdf

Cheung, Y.W. and Sengupta, R., 2013. Impact of exchange rate movements on exports: An analysis of Indian non-financial sector firms. *Journal of International Money and Finance, 39*, pp. 231–245.

Dhasmana, A., 2013. Transmission of real exchange rate changes to the manufacturing sector performance. IIM Bangalore Research Paper No. 435.

"Dumping of cheaper finished products cuts into scrap imports," October 2015 available at www.business-standard.com/article/markets/dumping-of-cheaper-finished-products-cuts-into-scrap-imports-115102700146_1.html

"End of textile quota regime: India must still spin faster to stay in place," September 2004 available at www.thehindubusinessline.com/2004/09/30/stories/2004093000061000.htm

"Environment and health in developing countries" (WHO), available at www.who.int/heli/risks/ehindevcoun/en/index1.html

EXIM, 2014. "Indian capital goods industry: A sector study," December 2014. EXIM Bank Occasional Paper No. 169.

"Export cheer from engineering goods," October 2014 available at www.business-standard.com/article/companies/export-cheer-from-engineering-goods-114100600739_1.html

Francis, S., 2015. *India's manufacturing sector export performance: A focus on missing domestic inter-sectoral linkages*. Institute for Studies in Industrial Development.

Gandhi, V.P. and Namboodiri, N.V., 2009. *Economics of BT Cotton vis-a-vis Non-BT cotton in India: A study across four major cotton growing states*. Centre for Management in Agriculture, Indian Institute of Management, Ahmedabad.

Gandhi, V.S. and Crawford, A., 2007. *Price volatility in the cotton yarn industry: Lessons from India*. International Institute for Sustainable Development.

Government of India (DSIR), 2015. *Textiles and garments: Export Price comparison*. DSIR.

Gulati, A. and Banerjee, P., 2015. Rationalising Fertiliser subsidy in India: Key issues and policy options. Working Paper No. 37.

Gulati, A., Jain, S., and Sharma, U., 2011. Indian Rice Landscape: Trade, Production and Government Intervention in Marketing. Paper presented at Kyushu University, Fukuoka, Japan (1 December).

"India iron ore imports hit record 6.8 mln tonnes as prices fall," December 2014 available at http://in.reuters.com/article/india-ironore-imports-idINKCN0JJ0EC20141205

"Indian diamond cutting and polishing sector," 2015 available at www.rough-polished.com/en/analytics/77889.html

"India's leather exports to take a hiding," 2014 available at http://wtocentre.iift.ac.in/ebulletin/India's%20Trade%20News%20and%20Views-%2024%20April%20to%208%20May%202014.pdf

"India wants EU to do away with import duty on its textiles," February 2016 available at http://articles.economictimes.indiatimes.com/2014-02-06/news/47089851_1_textiles-industry-textiles-sector-textiles-ministry

"Iron, steel exports plunge 41% to $4.57 billion in September," October 2015 available at http://economictimes.indiatimes.com/news/economy/foreign-trade/iron-steel-exports-plunge-41-to-4-57-billion-in-september/articleshow/49496795.cms

"Jewellery export might hit 4-year high in FY16," April 2015 available at www.business-standard.com/article/markets/jewellery-export-might-hit-4-year-high-in-fy16-115043001307_1.html

Keshari, P.K., 2012. Indian non-electrical machinery industry. MPRA Paper No. 43047 available at https://mpra.ub.uni-muenchen.de/43047/1/MPRA_paper_43047.pdf

Nagoor, B.H., 2009. Performance of India's tea exports: A comparative study of major tea exporting countries of the world. IGIDR Proceedings/Project Reports Series PP-062-21.

OECD-FAO Agricultural Outlook 2014, available at http://www.fao.org/3/a-i3818e.pdf.

"Pakistan's basmati export hopes fade; Indian prices fall," January 2016 available at www.thenews.com.pk/print/89561-Pakistans-basmati-export-hopes-fade-Indian-prices-fall

"Productivity and competitiveness of Indian manufacturing: Leather & Leather products sector," 2010, SIDBI available at http://nmcc.nic.in/pdf/Leather_03July2010.pdf

"Rajiv Kumar & Amitendu Palit: Has the fuel run out of India's exports?" February 2007 available at www.business-standard.com/article/opinion/rajiv-kumar-amitendu-palit-has-the-fuel-run-out-of-india-s-exports-107022601065_1.html

"Rice sales from India to reach record as Iran boosts," February 2014 Reserve available at www.bloomberg.com/news/articles/2014-02-13/rice-exports-from-india-climbing-to-record-on-mideast-demand

Sharma, V.P. and Thaker, H., 2011. *Demand for fertiliser in India: Determinants and outlook for 2020*. Indian Institute of Management.

Sharma, V.P. and Thaker, H., 2011. *Demand for fertiliser in India: Determinants and Outlook for 2020*. IIM Ahmedabad Working Paper Number 2011-04-01, available at www.iimahd.ernet.in/assets/snippets/workingpaperpdf/9641902932011-04-01.pdf

"Smelting Key to India's copper industry," October 2008 available at www.business-standard.com/article/markets/smelting-key-to-india-s-copper-industry-108100601028_1.html

"Steel makers approach government to look into dumping by foreign players," April 2015 available at http://articles.economictimes.indiatimes.com/2015-04-10/news/61017848_1_domestic-steel-manufacturers-steel-makers-tata-steel

Thorbecke, W., 2011. The effect of exchange rate changes on trade in East Asia. *Journal of International Commerce, Economics and Policy*, 2(1), pp. 85–102.

Chapter 4

Bilateral trade and exchange rates

Introduction

It is now amply clear that the impact of exchange rate movement on trade varies across types of commodities. For example, labour intensive commodities adjust to changes in the exchange rate whereas those within a value chain may not. In the earlier chapter, the major sources and destinations for each major item were identified. While this was to show market structures, this analysis may be flipped around to ask if bilateral trade, comprising a variety of commodities, too is sensitive to exchange rate movements, and if this impact depends on the kinds of commodities that comprise the trade basket. This issue is examined in top ten trading partners, for which the commodity composition is first shown and then a detailed statistical analysis undertaken.

Changes in direction of trade

Not only has the commodity composition of trade changed over time, so has the structure of bilateral trade. Broadly, the regional distribution of trade has transformed during the period 1980 to 2014. Share of exports going to countries in the Middle East and the developing countries in Asia has increased, whereas shares of the earlier dominant trade partners – the EU and the USA (Figure 4.1) – declined.

Similarly, for imports there has been a sharp decline in the share of imports from the advanced economies, including the EU. These declined from 60 per cent in 1998 to 35 per cent in 2013. On the other hand, the data indicate an increase in imports from developing Asia as well as from the Middle East. At this juncture, it may be useful to note that the decline in imports from the Middle East between 2000 and 2005 was perhaps due to the sourcing of oil from alternative sources. Therefore, in the same period, the share of unspecified countries went up. Subsequently, the share of imports from the Middle East countries recovered and, as of 2013, more than one-third of imports, comprising mainly of oil, are from the Middle East (Figure 4.2).

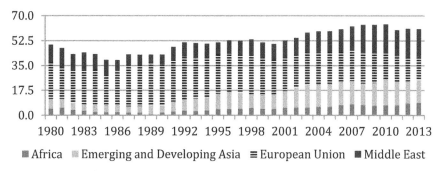

Figure 4.1 Region-wise share of exports (%)

Source: DoTS, IMF

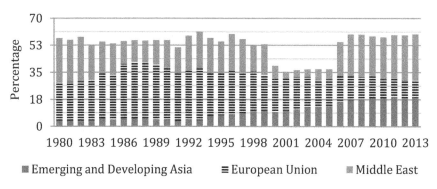

Figure 4.2 Region-wise share of imports

Source: DoTS, IMF

As was shown in the previous chapter, India exports major commodities to many countries. The top 20 countries accounted for approximately 70 per cent of all exports. While it is true that there are a few countries that account for a large fraction of India's exports, their shares have not remained unchanged. So the shares have churned over time, as is evident from the regional distribution. For example, the share of the USA, the single largest destination for exports, declined despite the increase in absolute value of exports during this period. A similar trend is observed for countries such as the UK, Japan, Germany, Italy, Hong Kong, and France. The decline observed for some major export destinations is due in part to relative rapid expansion of exports to the UAE. With a tenth of the exports directed to the UAE, it has gained prominence as the second largest market for India's exports. One of the reasons for such an increase may have been the growth of Dubai as one of the largest ports in the region and a centre for re-exports.

Another significant feature of India's trade is that exports to China emerged as an important market for India's exports. It is often suggested that growth of exports as well as growth of imports were the results of improved political and trade relations in the years after 2004, when India and China resumed border trade with opening up of the *silk road* (Bhattacharya and Bhattacharya, 2006: 3).

Among the developing countries to which India exports are three largest re-exporters, Hong Kong, Singapore, and the UAE. These three account for 20 per cent of all exports. Among developing Asian economies, which were earlier shown to have emerged as an important export market, are countries such as Vietnam. The majority of exports to Vietnam include primary items such as cotton and meat, both of which are India's revealed comparative advantage. The recent increase in exports to Vietnam can be attributed to the India-ASEAN agreement signed in August 2009 (Table 4A.1). A large part of this increase has been achieved through an increase in exports of items such as cotton, meat, and cereals. The other large Asian export market is Singapore. India exports manufactures to Singapore which include machinery and petroleum products to name a few.

The rise in the share of imports from developing Asia, shown earlier, resulted from the significant increase in imports from China. The previous chapter demonstrated that China accounts for the largest share of imports for most major commodities. Further, the Middle East remains the largest source of imports for India, despite the brief decline of imports for all countries between 2000 and 2005. Another important feature of India's bilateral imports has been a sharp decline in the share of imports from the USA. Over the period 1995 to 2013, the US share halved, even though in absolute terms, total imports from the USA continued to increase. The decline in the USA share can be attributed to relatively faster increase in imports from China, UAE, Saudi Arabia, and Switzerland.

Among the top countries from which India imports, a high degree of concentration in commodities has been observed. Nearly 90 per cent of all imports from Switzerland are of gold. In the cases of UAE and Saudi Arabia, as will be discussed later, the two major commodities are gold and crude oil. Therefore, the rapid increase in imports from the UAE and Switzerland is an indication of the growing share of gold and crude oil in the basket of imports. Given the large value of crude imports by India, the share of the OPEC countries has expanded over time. The decline in the share of the EU is apparent, as the large trading partners within the EU – Germany, Belgium, the UK, and Italy – all displayed decline in shares of imports between 1995 and 2013.

The improvement in bilateral relations between India and China has opened up trade between the countries that resulted in the emergence of

Table 4.1 Share in exports (%) and value of exports (US$ million)

Country	1995		2000		2005		2013	
	Share of exports	Value of exports (US$ million)	Share of exports	Value of exports (US$ million)	Share of exports	Value of exports (US$ million)	Share of exports	Value of exports (US$ million)
United States	17.4	5,305	21.3	9,083	16.8	16,475	12.3	38,711
United Arab Emirates	4.3	1,306	5.8	2,469	8.4	8,281	10.1	31,957
China	0.9	283	1.8	758	6.6	6,473	4.6	14,517
Singapore	2.6	807	1.9	826	5.2	5,069	4.3	13,479
Hong Kong	6	1821	6.1	2,608	4.4	4,276	4.1	13,024
Saudi Arabia	1.4	425	1.9	803	1.7	1,710	3.7	11,793
United Kingdom	6.2	1,881	5.2	2,233	4.8	4,715	3.1	9,625
Netherlands	2.3	711	2.1	882	2.3	2,257	2.7	8,591
Germany	6	1,841	4.4	1,865	3.5	3,396	2.4	7,427
Japan	7	2,130	4.1	1,767	2.4	2,393	2.1	6,764
Belgium	0	0	3.4	1,445	2.8	2,781	2	6,328
Bangladesh	3.1	960	2	860	1.7	1,656	1.8	5,710
Brazil	0.3	98	0.5	203	1	988	1.7	5,413
South Africa	0.9	269	0.7	304	1.4	1,391	1.7	5,265
Vietnam	0.3	97	0.5	208	0.7	657	1.7	5,303
France	2.2	683	2.3	999	2	1,996	1.6	5,190
Indonesia	1.6	501	0.9	386	1.4	1,368	1.6	5,197
Iran	0.5	160	0.5	208	1.2	1,199	1.6	4,944
Russian Federation	3.4	1,031	2.1	904	0.7	708	0.7	2,213
Italy	3.2	974	3	1,262	2.5	2,461	1.6	5,099
Thailand	1.5	461	1.2	510	1.1	1,032	1.2	3,906
Korea, Republic of	1.3	394	1.1	457	1.7	1,631	1.3	4,099
Sri Lanka	1.3	383	1.4	605	1.9	1,872	1.3	4,227
Total	73.7	22,521	74.2	31,646	76.2	74,785	69.2	218,780

Source: DoTS, IMF

China as a major trading partner for India. The decline in the share of the EU for both exports and imports has been sharp, primarily on account of decline for two countries – the UK and Germany.

Although it is true that the share of the EU has declined, it continues to be the largest trading partner with a share of exports at 17 per cent and

Table 4.2 Share in imports (%) and value of imports (US$ million)

Country	1995		2000		2005		2013	
	Share of imports	Value of exports (US$ million)	Share of imports	Value of exports (US$ million)	Share of imports	Value of exports (US$ million)	Share of imports	Value of exports (US$ million)
China	2	811	3	1,449	7	9,926	11	51,456
Saudi Arabia	5	1,860	2	1,220	1	1,550	8	36,083
United Arab Emirates	5	1,594	2	1,078	3	4,426	7	33,214
Switzerland	2	787	6	3,020	5	6,403	6	25,797
United States	10	3,344	6	3,152	6	8,848	5	23,480
Iraq	0	0	0	55	0	2	4	19,666
Kuwait	5	1,884	1	563	0	423	4	17,534
Germany	8	2,713	4	1,780	4	5,522	3	13,543
Indonesia	1	384	2	922	2	2,911	3	15,232
Korea, Republic of	2	717	2	989	3	4,300	3	12,453
Nigeria	2	629	2	780	0	66	3	12,851
Qatar	0	98	0	112	1	844	3	14,447
Venezuela	0	10	0	11	0	8	3	14,919
Australia	3	945	2	1,068	3	4,667	2	11,094
Belgium	0	0	6	3,073	3	4,691	2	10,560
Hong Kong	1	242	2	844	1	2,088	2	7,920
Iran	2	574	1	471	0	629	2	10,028
Japan	6	2,234	4	2,016	3	3,855	2	10,541
United Kingdom	5	1,683	6	3,053	3	3,839	1	6,501
Italy	3	888	1	726	1	1,735	1	4,243
Singapore	3	966	3	1,482	2	3,178	1	6,997
Bahrain	2.3	794	0.5	246	0.1	173	0.1	578
Malaysia	2	770	3	1,389	2	2,386	2	9,061
Total	74	25,508	59	29,496	50	72,469	78	368,199

Source: DoTS, IMF

share of imports at 10.8 per cent in 2014. The other trading partner that has lost out in terms of share in trade is the USA. Therefore, it can be said that the structure of trade has transformed over time even in terms of trading partners.

China, Hong Kong, the USA, UAE, Saudi Arabia, the UK, Germany, Belgium, the Netherlands, Singapore, and Switzerland are selected for analysis in this chapter.

Does the exchange rate matter for bilateral trade?

Sufficient evidence has been provided to show that the exchange rate and trade interactions are nuanced and vary across commodity markets. The trade with major trading partners is also expected to be structurally diverse. As a result, it may be asked whether exchange rate is a tool that can influence bilateral trade. The equations estimated are as follows:

$$logexports = \alpha + \beta_1 logreal\,exchange\,rate + \beta_2 GDP\,of\,trading\,partner$$

$$logimports = \alpha + \beta_1 logreal\,exchange\,rate + \beta_2 India's GDP \qquad (4.1)$$

These equations are estimated for the period 1990–2014[1] for each of the trading partners. Note that the measures of real effective exchange rate have been used for estimation. The estimated coefficients for the exchange rate appear in Table 4.3 (for full results, check the Appendix, Table 4A.2). The estimates provided in Table 4.3 have been checked for robustness where the issues of autocorrelation and heteroskedasticity have been taken care of.

From Table 4.3 it is seen that there are countries where the exchange rate is found to have an impact on exports whereas there are others where no such impact is observed. On the other hand, for most countries imports do not respond as is expected. While for some countries they are seen to expand (decline), in rupee terms, with depreciation (appreciation), for others no impact is observed.

Table 4.3 Estimated coefficient for real exchange rate

Country	Exports	Imports
Belgium	−0.9	−2.54
China	−5.08	−6.46
Germany	0	0
Hong Kong	−2.37	−2.2
Japan	0	0
Netherlands	0	0
Saudi Arabia	0	0
Singapore	0	0
Switzerland	_	−4.15
UAE	−2.64	0
UK	−0.95	−1.83
USA	−1.05	0

Note: "0" implies it was insignificant; "_" implies that it was not estimated because it is not a major export destination.

Source: All tables are estimated based on author's fieldwork unless otherwise mentioned.

The countries where the exchange rate has no impact on exports are Germany, Japan, the Netherlands, Saudi Arabia,[2] and Singapore. Pre-empting the discussion in the subsequent sections for the commodity disaggregation of bilateral trade, it is verified whether concentration of petroleum products seems to be the reason for a lack of response observed the case of these countries, where the exchange rate does not seem to have any significant impact. For countries such as Saudi Arabia, Japan, the Netherlands, and Singapore, it is observed that over time petroleum products have emerged as a significant proportion of total exports. Therefore, in order to further build a case for commodity disaggregation of bilateral trade, the equation is estimated for non-oil exports for all countries where the exchange rate was found to be insignificant. It is found that other than for Singapore, the exclusion of petroleum products from exports does not change the results. One implication of this result is that while petroleum component does influence the results, there may be other commodities that determine the direction of the impact of the exchange rate on trade. To better understand the underlying causes for the direction of impact, bilateral trade is further disaggregated by commodity.

The difference in response to exchange rates: is it commodity composition?[3]

USA

Two major structural changes occurred during the period 2000–14 with respect to trade with the USA. The first was that the share of apparel in exports halved over the period. Second, there was a phenomenal increase in exports of pharmaceuticals. Expansion in the share of export of products such as pharmaceuticals, from a mere 0.6 per cent in 2000 to 7.25 per cent in 2014, and of machinery, from 5 per cent to 10 per cent, was accompanied by a contraction in shares of commodities such as gems and jewellery (from 34% to 19%) and apparel (from 20% to 12%). The other major commodities with modest rates of growth were petroleum products (3.8%) and organic chemicals (5%).

There was also diversification in the product composition of exports to the USA. More categories of manufactures, including organic chemicals and machinery were exported in 2014 than were in 2000. As for imports from the USA, the commodity composition has remained more or less the same over the period 2000–14. Machinery has remained among the largest import over this period, although the share declined from 35 per cent in 2000 to 20 per cent in 2014. Import of other major items such as fertilisers has increased in value, whereas its share in imports has remained the same, around 2 per cent. Similarly, import of organic chemicals that consist of dyeing, tanning, and colouring materials has increased steadily in absolute terms.

On the other hand, growth in imports of gems and jewellery consisting of precious stones and gold (16% of imports in 2014), aircraft equipment (10%), and coke (7%) overshadowed the growth in imports of other commodities. India is a major source of polished diamonds for the USA, while India imports gold from the USA. Since exports and imports in this category have expanded between the two countries, given that India is an important source of small and large diamonds for the USA, India runs a trade surplus in this category (Figure 4.3).

The change in product composition has been observed for exports and imports during the period 1990–2014. This shift has been such that the structures are largely similar for these exports and imports where gems and jewellery, machinery, and chemicals form a large fraction.

In the years preceding the global financial crisis, USA demand for India was stable, as was the demand for imports from the USA. However after the crisis, the USA's demand for Indian exports declined in 2010, which manifested in a decline in the quantum of exports. At the same time, the quantum of imports declined at a similar rate such that even though the two declined, the Qx/Qm ratio remained more or less stable for the period. The changes in quantities of exports and imports are strongly associated with changes in the level of activity measured by income or trade globally. On the other hand, relative price of tradables or net terms of trade were stable or increasing until 2008, and thereafter it declined. The decline in the quantity and relative price of exports had an adverse impact on the trade position. In 2008 and 2009, the trade surplus with the USA declined, recovering only after 2010.

While analysing the trends in relative price and quantity indices, it is seen that the two have moved in opposite directions throughout the period (Figure 4.4). This is indicative of a decline (rise) in quantity with an increase (decrease) in prices. Such movements in price and quantity suggest that the change in price of tradables as a consequence of change in exchange rate would result in a quantity adjustment.

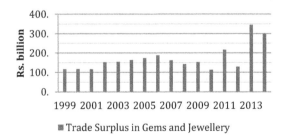

Figure 4.3 Trade surplus in gems and jewellery (Rs. billion)

Source: DGCIS

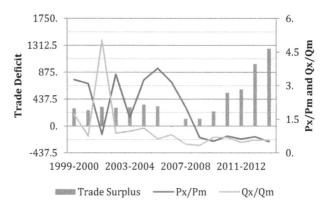

Figure 4.4 Terms of trade and trade deficit (Rs. billion) with the USA

Source: Computed from DGCIS

Since exports to the USA consist mostly of commodities (pharmaceuticals, apparel, machinery, and gems and jewellery) that were shown to respond to changes in the exchange rate in the previous chapter, a similar result is found to exist for bilateral exports. That is, exchange rate depreciation (appreciation) leads to an expansion (a reduction) in exports to the USA (Table 4.3). On the other hand, the imports from the USA consist of products such as chemicals, petroleum (which includes coke), and gems and jewellery, all of which were shown to be unresponsive to the exchange rate. Thus, imports from the USA do not respond to changes in the exchange rate.

UAE

The UAE has emerged as a major trading partner for India. The significance of India-UAE trade is reflected in the equally large share of India in UAE's trade. In 2014, India's share in UAE's imports was 13.3 per cent while that of UAE in India's exports was 10.44 per cent.

India's exports to the UAE are concentrated in two items – gems and jewellery, and petroleum products. These two contribute 57 per cent to exports and 84 per cent to imports.

The emergence of the UAE as an important trading partner is often associated with its rise as a major trading hub with free trade zones that have attracted some of the Indian companies, particularly from sectors such as oil and gas (for example, IOC). A large part of exports that reach the UAE, including gems and jewellery, is re-exported to other Gulf countries.[4] It is to be noted that the exports and imports are similar in commodity composition.

Gems and jewellery have remained among the top items of exports from India to the UAE, Imports from the UAE consist largely of gold and precious stones. These were a third of total imports. The importance of the UAE for supply of crude is well known. However, now India also exports refined products to the UAE. The creation of refining capacity in India has resulted in exports of petroleum products to the UAE. Last, apparel,[5] another major item of export to the UAE, has witnessed slower growth (as was mentioned in the earlier chapter), which resulted in a decline of its share from 20 per cent in 2000 to 7 per cent in 2014. Therefore, the trade with UAE is largely in labour intensive products and minerals.

Even though India imports crude from the UAE, the fact that it has been able to export more of gems and jewellery and cereals has allowed it to maintain a trade surplus with the UAE. Further, India exports iron and steel, machinery, apparel, aircraft equipment, copper, and cereals[6] that further contribute to the trade surplus. However, in 2010 there was a reversal in this trend. The balance of trade slid into a deficit that lasted for the following two years. The deficit was the result of relatively slow growth in exports of gems and jewellery, and the expansion of the oil import bill owing to the rise in oil prices.[7] The rise in price of imports, attributable to oil prices, can be seen by the sharp dip in net terms of trade. Subsequently, the net terms of trade improved and the surplus position was regained.

Looking at the overall trends, over the period 2000–14, the fast expansion of imports is reflected in the decline in Qx/Qm, whereas the price of exports rose faster such that the net terms of trade improved. The increase in the latter has, in turn, contributed to a rise in trade surplus, in spite of adverse quantity adjustments. Looking at the strong co-movement in the price and quantity in Figure 4.5, it is possible that there are quantity adjustments in response to exchange rate changes.

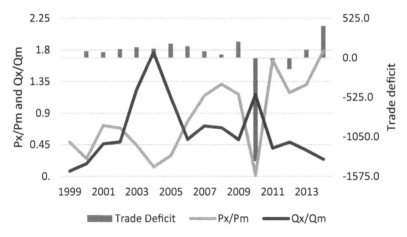

Figure 4.5 Terms of trade and trade deficit (Rs. billion) with UAE

Source: Computed from DGCIS

The discussion of product composition throws light on the fact that exports to the UAE are concentrated in labour intensive goods. As a result, the estimated coefficient for the exchange rate shows that there is an increase (decrease) in exports with depreciation (appreciation). As for imports, given that crude forms a major proportion of imports along with items of gems and jewellery, including gold, the exchange rate has no impact on imports.

With UAE's emergence as a major trading hub, it may seek to expand bilateral trade[8] with India. This offers a lucrative prospect to India, since it can expand its market for exports that are its revealed comparative advantage such as cereals, gems, and jewellery. Exchange rate movements, as it seems, can play a role in achieving the goal.

Hong Kong

The share of Hong Kong exports has declined marginally, from 6 per cent to 4.1 per cent over 2000–14, while the share of imports from Hong Kong has remained the same. Both exports and imports exhibit a high degree of concentration. Sixty-six per cent of imports and 89 per cent of exports in 2014 consisted of gems and jewellery. Other items of exports to Hong Kong included raw hide (3%) and electrical machinery (1.6%). Similarly, on the import side, other than gems and jewellery, the other major item is electrical machinery, which contributes 16 per cent to imports. Yet again, there is high degree of similarity in the composition of exports and imports.

During the period of analysis, it is seen that the quantity of exports increased, though at a much slower rate than that of imports until 2006, after which there was a reversal in the trend. This increase in imports was associated with the large increase in export of diamonds, for which Hong Kong now is the third largest importer (Mukherjee and Mukherjee, 2012). On the other hand, net terms of trade that remained high until 2007 collapsed in the period after the global financial crisis. This adverse movement in the net terms of trade, attributable to the sharp increase in price of imports of rough diamonds[9] and gold, resulted in the shrinking of the trade surplus with Hong Kong. Nevertheless, the surplus position was maintained throughout the period. Hence, quantity movements have a significant bearing on the trade position, which in turn are affected by price movements (Figure 4.6).

Given that exports are concentrated in labour intensive products, depreciation (appreciation) of the exchange rate results in an increase (decrease) in exports.

The imports show a similar level of concentration as exports, where the precious stones are the single largest item of import. Given the fact that a single commodity dominates imports and this product is an important input to the gems and jewellery sector, imports increase with depreciation, thereby suggesting inelasticity.

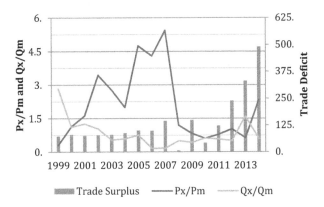

Figure 4.6 Terms of trade and trade deficit (Rs. billion) with Hong Kong

Source: Computed from DGCIS

Saudi Arabia

The other country from the Middle East to have emerged as India's top export destinations is Saudi Arabia, with a share of 8 per cent of exports in 2014. While Saudi Arabia has always been an important source of crude imports except for the brief suspension of trade during 2000 to 2004, other commodities, such as organic chemicals and plastics, are imported by India from Saudi Arabia. The composition of imports has remained unchanged over the period of analysis, with more than 80 per cent of the imports comprising of the aforementioned three products.

The structure of exports to Saudi Arabia has, however, changed over time. Articles of apparel that in 2000 contributed to 14 per cent of exports dwindled to 5 per cent in 2014. Petroleum products emerged as the largest item of export to Saudi Arabia (22% in 2014). The rise of export of petroleum products to crude-exporting countries has been the result of the creation of excess refining capacity, as was mentioned earlier in the case of UAE.

Saudi Arabia is also amongst the largest markets for India's rice exports. Though exports of cereals have halved in share, attributable mostly to phenomenal increase in petroleum exports, it has remained the second largest product exported to Saudi Arabia in 2014 (14%), followed by machinery (9%) and meat (3.8%). Last, exports to Saudi Arabia also exhibit a certain degree of concentration, where seven items account for 70 per cent of all exports, though it is not comparable to that for UAE and Hong Kong.

While there is diversity in the product basket of exports, with primary, mineral as well as labour intensive products among the top exports, imports are heavily concentrated in crude. Further, the growth in quantity of imports owing to a rise in demand for crude resulted in a consistent trade deficit shown in Figure 4.7(a).

Though the improvements in net terms of trade in 2009 and 2014 did result in slight improvement in the trade deficit with Saudi Arabia, nevertheless the increase in quantity of imports has left a wider deficit over time. From Figures 4.7(a) and 4.7(b), it is evident that the quantities do not seem to move with price. Therefore, a poor quantity adjustment is expected.

The fact that exports to Saudi Arabia consist of a wide array of products that are largely in category of commodities for which the exchange rate does not have any impact is reflected in the results for estimated coefficient. Similarly, the dominance of petroleum products in the imports corroborates the lack of impact of the exchange rate on imports from Saudi Arabia.

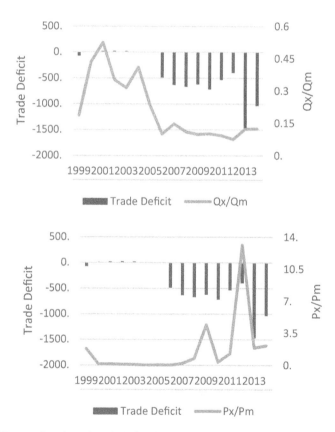

Figure 4.7 Terms of trade and trade deficit (Rs. billion) with Saudi Arabia

Source: Computed from DGCIS

Singapore

Among Asian economies, Singapore is India's second largest trading partner after China. In 2014, its share of exports was 4.3 per cent, while its share in imports was a little over 1 per cent. The growth in trade between these two countries was bolstered by the signing of the Comprehensive Economic Cooperation Agreement (CECA) in August 2005. While exports had been increasing across the period, the increase in imports was rather sharp after the signing of the CECA (Figure 4.8).

As a part of the agreement, customs duties were removed on 506 items, which included electronic goods, organic chemicals, and machinery (Palit, 2008: 6). There is also evidence that Indian exporters increased their exports to ASEAN through Singapore, owed to the duty benefit (Palit, 2008). Therefore, some exports to Singapore are meant for transshipment and hence, some of the increase in exports to Singapore can be taken as an indication of an increase in exports to the rest of Asia.

The structure of exports has gone through a significant change over the period 2000–14. Items such as aluminium and articles made of aluminium, iron and steel, and cotton, which were among the top ten exports in 2000, declined both in terms of share and value. The shares of machinery and gems and jewellery in total exports also declined; however, these still remain among the largest items of export to Singapore. The decline in shares of these commodities was accompanied by growth in export of petroleum products. In fact, this growth was so sharp that there was an increase in concentration of exports such that petroleum products account for as much as 54 per cent of exports to Singapore.

Other than petroleum, export of ships, boats, and floating structures registered a significant increase in share from 0.9 per cent to 9 per cent. On the import side, the degree of concentration as well as the commodity structure has remained more or less the same. The imports comprise machinery, which were replaced by organic chemicals as the largest

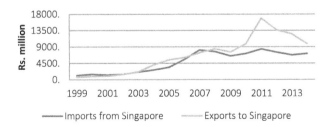

Figure 4.8 Exports to and imports from Singapore (Rs. million)

Source: DGCIS

item of import in 2014 (20%). These included items that are exempt from customs. There has also been an increase in the share and value of imports of crude, ships, boats, and floating structures as well as gems and jewellery.

Observing the structure of trade with Singapore, it can be said that the concentration of exports has increased with an increase in the share of petroleum, and there has been a slight increase in similarity between exports and imports. The similarity can be attributed to the trade in products such as machinery, ships, boats, and floating structures.

The net terms of trade have been volatile but increasing between 2000 and 2014, whereas the quantity of imports increased over this period. The movements in net terms of trade and Qx/Qm have together determined the value of deficit or surplus, and for most years the two have tended to move in opposite directions. For example, in 2012 the sharp decline in net terms of trade was accompanied by a rise of Qx/Qm that, in turn, led to a trade surplus (Figure 4.9).

Even though the quantity moves in the opposite direction from that of the prices, the response to changes in price is weaker, therefore indicating weaker adjustment in quantity. As was shown in the earlier section, while for the overall exports the result seems to be driven by the petroleum exports, the sign flips when petroleum exports are excluded. For the remaining exports which consist of items such as machinery, gems and jewellery, ships, boats, floating structures, and aircraft equipment,[10] the exchange rate is shown to have a significant impact, a result substantiated by the commodity-wise estimates. The imports, on the other hand, picked up after the signing of CECA. Therefore, in the case of imports, it is shown that exchange rate has no significant impact, especially since the agreement waived off customs on imports of some items.

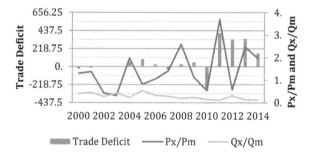

Figure 4.9 Terms of trade and trade deficit (in Rs. billion) with Singapore

Source: Computed from DGCIS

United Kingdom

Trade with the UK has been on a decline over the years 2000 to 2014. Its share in exports and imports halved over the period. The product composition of exports remained largely unchanged whereas that of imports witnessed a significant change.

The EU is a major market for India's apparel exports of which the UK constitutes a significant portion. In 2014, 36 per cent of apparel exports to the EU were to the UK and accounted for 20 per cent of exports to the UK. The other products that India exports to the UK are machinery (12.5%), gems and jewellery (5.5%). and footwear (5.3%). Thus, the UK provides a market for India's labour intensive exports.

The change in composition has also been observed for imports, which in 2000 were concentrated in gems and jewellery, with a share close to 70 per cent that declined to 23 per cent in 2014. This decline in share was accompanied by a similar decline in absolute value. There was also a change in the product mix within gems and jewellery imports. While in 2000 these largely consisted of precious stones, in 2014 these consisted predominantly of silver. In the recent period the UK Office of National Statistics has reported that there was an increase in *erratic exports* of the UK, which includes items such as silver for which India provides a large market, given the size of its gems and jewellery market.[11] India also imports machinery from the UK, the share of which has more than doubled over the period of analysis (from 9% in 2000 to 20% in 2014).

Unlike other trading partners, the composition of exports and imports differ. While India predominantly exports labour intensive commodities, it imports products that are capital intensive. The dominance of labour intensive commodities that are among India's revealed comparative advantage is a positive feature of trade with the UK. The commodities imported by India consist of items such as precious metal and machinery that command a higher value, shown by the decline in net terms of trade after 2006.

The relative price of exports and the relative quantity of import increased between 2004 and 2007, after which a decline was observed for both. The period of increase did reverse the deficit that had persisted in the preceding years, i.e. between 1999 and 2004. However, the sharp decline in prices and quantity, especially the former in 2010, resulted in a large trade deficit. In the subsequent years, the upward movement in quantity adjustments resulted in rise in trade surplus (Figure 4.10).

As is expected, the predominance of labour intensive exports is an explanation for the observed impact of exchange rate movement on bilateral exports, whereas the capital intensive nature of imports are shown to be price inelastic. That is, exchange rate depreciation leads to higher value of imports.

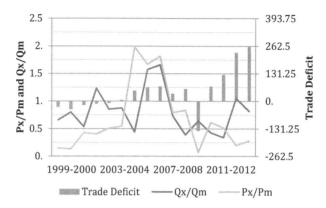

Figure 4.10 Terms of trade and trade deficit (in Rs. billion) with the UK

Source: Computed from DGCIS

Germany

The decline in the share of trade with the EU is reflected in the trend observed for each of the EU countries. The share of exports to Germany halved over the period 2000–14. As mentioned earlier, the EU is an important market for India's apparel exports, and that is true also for exports to Germany. These consist largely of apparel, and in this regard, while the value of exports have expanded over time, the share has remained approximately the same over this period (16.2% in 2014). The EU is also an important market for India's leather export, although over time it has lost out in the market due to better quality leather exported by China and imposition of ban on imports from India by the EU countries. Despite such challenges, leather products remain among the largest exports to Germany (5% in 2014). In addition, India also exported carpets and footwear, which contributed 1.8% and 5.1% of total exports respectively to Germany in 2014. Though the share of labour intensive exports declined over the period (from 45.4% to 32.4%), these continue to contribute up to a third of exports. There has also been a simultaneous increase in exports of heavy industry exports such as machinery (14%), organic chemicals (8%), and vehicles and accessories (4%).

On the import side, however, the structure of trade has remained unchanged over the years. There has also been a concentration in imports where machinery contributes close to 40 per cent of total imports. Other than machinery, organic chemicals and vehicles (or parts thereof) contribute more than 11 per cent. Exports to Germany consist of a mix of labour intensive and capital intensive commodities.

India has consistently run a trade deficit with Germany, and its expansion, during the period of analysis, is explained by the decline in both net

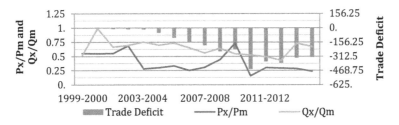

Figure 4.11 Terms of trade and trade deficit (in Rs. billion) with Germany

Source: Computed from DGCIS

terms of trade and the relative quantity of exports. That is, the price and quantity of imports have expanded relatively fast so as to result in a higher deficit over time (Figure 4.11).

The quantity response to changes in price seems to be weak for Germany over the entire period. Moreover, the composition of exports has changed where the share of commodities such as footwear, carpets,[12] chemicals, and vehicles has increased over time. For these commodities, the exchange rate does not have any significant influence on exports. On the other hand, there are other commodities such as apparel and machinery for which exchange rate depreciation leads to an increase in exports. Therefore, an equal share[13] of commodities that are sensitive to the exchange rate as those which are not gives a coefficient that is of the right sign but is insignificant. Similarly, the commodity composition of imports justifies the lack of response observed for imports from Germany.

Japan

Japan is among the countries for which a decline in the share of trade has been observed for the period 2000 to 2014. Japan's share in exports as well as imports in 2014 was a third of what it was in 1995. Over this period, the product composition of exports has changed in many ways. One, fish and crustaceans, an item that was the largest export with a share of 28.2 per cent in 2000, declined to 8 per cent in 2014. While it still remains the second largest commodity exported to Japan, the rate of growth of exports has been close to zero. The decline in exports of fish to Japan has much to do with the change in preferences. In the last decade, the consumption of fish in Japan has declined to the extent that the country has switched from being the largest importer of seafood to an exporter of seafood.[14] The second important change in product composition was that exports of petroleum products went from a negligible 0.5 per cent in 2000 to a substantial

34.7 per cent in 2014. In spite of the growth in exports of petroleum, such an increase still remains marginal from the point of view of Japan. Japan relies significantly on domestic production,[15] thus the increase in exports to Japan that can be realised through export of petroleum is limited. Third, exports of gems and jewellery too declined over the period. The share of this commodity in exports declined from 21.5 per cent to 5.3 per cent. The primary reason for such decline was the reduction in demand on account of a slowdown.[16]

To summarise, the concentration of exports to Japan has declined over time, and there has been a change in commodities that constitute a major share. Fish and gems and jewellery that consisted of 50 per cent of exports are now replaced by other commodities such as petroleum products. Other than these few commodities, ores, iron and steel, machinery, vehicles (and parts thereof), and organic chemicals, though relatively small, have increased over time.

The structure of imports has remained largely unchanged, with machinery at 35 per cent constituting a major share of exports in 2014. India also imports other items such as organic chemicals and measuring apparatus. The only major change has been the increase in imports of iron and steel from Japan. The signing of CEPA with Japan in 2011, as was discussed in Chapter 3, has had an adverse impact on the iron and steel market in India, where the finished product competes with cheaper imports. In fact, breaking down trade in this segment further, it is observed that India exports pig iron and iron ore concentrates to Japan, and it imports flat rolled products of alloy from Japan. Therefore, the nature of commodities traded is such that India provides raw material to import finished products, which is problematic given that there are reports of excess capacity in the steel production in India.[17]

While India still exports a large proportion of mineral-based commodities to Japan, there has been some increase in share of exports of manufactures. At the same time, India imports manufactures from Japan within the same category of goods as it exports. It is important to make note of this feature because, as with Singapore, trade consists of manufactures between the countries, a possible sign of shift in structure of trade with Asia in favour of manufacturing.

The Qx/Qm ratio shown in Figure 4.12 reflects relative decline in exports. As for the net terms of trade, after the sharp decline between 2003 and 2005, it recovered and remained stable. Therefore, the decline in the quantity of exports with relatively stable imports has manifested in an increase in the trade deficit.

Quantity and price have tended to move in opposite directions in some of the years such as 2003–04, 2005–06, and 2009–10. The possibility of quantity adjustment may be observed for some years; however, it is seen that overall for this period, exports and imports are unresponsive to changes

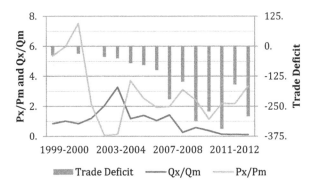

Figure 4.12 Terms of trade and trade deficit (in Rs. billion) with Japan

Source: Computed from DGCIS

in exchange rate. The cause for no impact can be attributed to commodity composition wherein exports to Japan consist of commodities – organic chemicals, vehicles, fish, and petroleum – which are not sensitive to movements in exchange rate. Imports from Japan have declined over the period and now consist of items – ores, chemicals, electrical machinery, and vehicles – where no impact of the exchange rate is observed.

Netherlands

Contrary to the trend observed for most countries of the EU, the share of exports to the Netherlands has remained more or less stable, around 2 per cent over the period 2000–14. The composition of exports, however, has changed significantly over time. The importance of apparel in the basket of exports remains a common feature across the EU. However, the other products that India exports to the Netherlands are distinctly different from the rest of the EU.

In 2000 India's export of apparel was 17 per cent of exports to the Netherlands, followed by items such as edible fruits, nuts, etc. (10%); leather products (1.8%); and machinery (7%). However, in 2014, petroleum overtook apparel as the largest item of export. This increase was accompanied by a growth in concentration of exports, where petroleum exports contributed 39 per cent. Inorganic chemicals (6.2%) and machinery (7%), though far less in share as compared to petroleum, are also among the other major items of export. While the Netherlands is a major destination for India's exports, India does not rely significantly on the Netherlands for its imports, and its share in India's imports is very low.[18] India thus runs a trade surplus with Netherlands. The quantities of exports and imports have remained

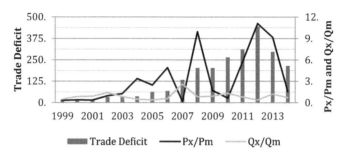

Figure 4.13 Terms of trade and trade deficit (in Rs. billion) with the Netherlands

Source: Computed from DGCIS

stable over the period, whereas the price of exports have increased sporadically. As a result, the trade surplus has expanded from time to time with improvements in net terms of trade.

The changes in quantity for most years, with the exception of 2007, 2008 and 2010, was shown to be weak in response to change in prices (as shown in Figure 4.13) for Netherlands. This can be attributed to the structural change in exports, where there has been an increase in concentration owed to petroleum products that contribute close to 40 per cent. As was mentioned earlier, the exclusion of the petroleum component does not change the estimated coefficient. The lack of impact observed even after exclusion of the petroleum products can be explained by the predominance of commodities such as chemicals, leather, and edible fruits that are not sensitive to exchange rate changes. Though apparel remains among the top exports to the Netherlands, they now form a small part of exports. Therefore, the exchange rate is seen to have no impact on exports. For the imports as well, the exchange rate is found to be insignificant.

Belgium

Belgium is amongst the EU countries that holds a significant share in India's trade. Belgium holds an equal share of exports as it does of imports (2%). Moreover the share has remained approximately the same over the period 2000–14.

The product composition of exports has remained concentrated, where gems and jewellery contributed 48 per cent to India's exports in 2014. These mainly consist of polished diamonds. Further, organic chemicals, iron and steel, fish, and tobacco have replaced exports of cotton and apparel among the top five exports. Therefore, there has been some product diversification in exports.

As for imports, the concentration is comparatively higher than that for exports, with more than 80 per cent of imports consisting of precious stones. As is known, Belgium exports rough diamonds that are polished in India and then re-exported. Therefore, Belgium has been an important trading partner for the gems and jewellery sector.

Even though India has diversified its product basket for exports with Belgium, its exports consist predominantly of labour intensive and primary commodities. The high degree of similarity in exports and imports has probably been the cause for the stable net terms of trade. However, after 2006, the Qx/Qm ratio has declined. This decline, given stable unit values for most of the period, has resulted in the worsening of the trade balance (Figure 4.14). In fact, the trade deficit is driven by items such as gems and jewellery for which the deficit exceeds the overall. The deficit has been reigned in to some extent by product diversification (Figure 4.15).

When the movements in Px/Pm and Qx/Qm are observed for the period 1999 to 2014, it is seen that throughout the period, prices and quantities

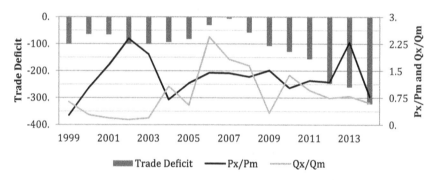

Figure 4.14 Terms of trade and trade deficit (in Rs. billion) with Belgium

Source: Computed form DGCIS

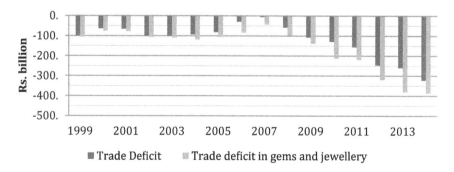

Figure 4.15 Exports and imports of gems and jewellery (Rs. billion) with Belgium

Source: DGCIS

have moved in opposite directions and the movements in quantity have been equally large as those in prices. Therefore, quantity adjustments are expected to result from changes in exchange rate (that have an impact on prices). Again, the product composition helps to predict the results. A large share of labour intensive products results in an estimated coefficient as per which the exchange rate deprecation (appreciation) leads to higher (lower) value of exports.

The imports consist primarily of precious stones. Since Belgium is the largest source of diamonds for India and the output of the gems and jewellery sector depends on the import of diamonds, depreciation (appreciation) leads to higher (lower) value of imports.

China

As trade with China picked up during the period 1990–2014, the structure of trade changed. In 1999, India's exports to China consisted predominantly of iron ore (20%), fish and crustaceans (16.2%), organic chemicals (12%), and cotton (10%). However, in 2014, the largest item of export to China was cotton (19%), followed by copper (16%), petroleum products (11%), and organic chemicals (9.4%). The decline in exports of iron ore and fish was not only in terms of share, but also in terms of value. The decline in exports of iron ore that began in 2012 came primarily as a result of the crackdown on illegal mining in India, a precursor to the government ban on mining in Goa and Karnataka. In Goa, 90 mines account for more than 50 per cent of iron ore exports. Therefore, the temporary suspension affected exports adversely.[19] Soon after, China began sourcing more of its iron ore demand from other countries, including Australia and Brazil.[20] On the other hand, export of fish and crustaceans declined with the introduction of new regulations in 2011 that governed the imports of seafood into China. As per the guidelines, the imports would have to be accompanied by inspection certificates approved by the quarantine authority. The impact of further regulatory revisions in 2012 was felt far and wide, and this category of exports no longer had a place in the top ten commodities of export.[21]

On the other hand, the growth in exports of copper and copper products to China showed a significant increase. The other item of export that constitutes a large proportion is cotton. The growth in apparel exports from China was accompanied by an increase in Chinese imports of cotton from India. What emerges from the structure of exports to China is that while India does export machinery to China (8% in 2014), growth in these exports has not been as rapid as that for commodities such as copper and cotton.

On the other hand, imports from China have largely remained the same in terms of composition, with categories such as machinery and organic chemicals securing their spot as the top imports. Imports of machinery have shown a consistent rise in terms of value as well as in terms of share; the data indicate that the share of machinery in imports from China rose from 22 per cent in 2000 to 41 per cent in 2014. While organic chemicals declined in terms of share of imports, they increased in absolute terms. Import of fertilisers from China has increased over time, and even though these account for 5 per cent of the Chinese exports to India, these constitute 50 per cent of India's import demand for fertiliser. In the recent period there has also been a substantial increase in imports of iron and steel from China. The import of steel at competitive prices has been a cause of concern to the domestic producers who fear being priced out of the market.[22] The other dramatic change was for commodities such as mineral fuels and silk that declined substantially in shares and value over time. The decline in silk imports was the result of the domestic boom in silk output that began in 2008–09.[23] Imports of mineral fuels like coke, though, have been volatile over the period; coke is among the largest items. The import of coke, too, has been at prices that can potentially render domestic production uncompetitive.[24]

The comparison of the structures of exports and imports brings out an important feature of the trade between India and China. While India still exports many primary or mineral-based commodities to China, India's imports consist of manufactures such as machinery and organic chemicals.

Taking the top ten items, the categories of organic chemicals and machinery (electrical and non-electrical) are common for exports to and imports from China. While India now increasingly exports machinery and organic chemicals to China, it runs a deficit in both these commodities, which have expanded over time (Figure 4.16). The net terms

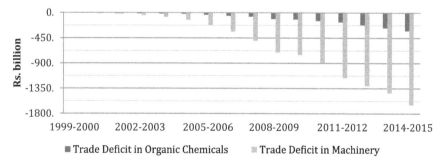

Figure 4.16 Trade deficit in organic chemicals with China (in Rs. billion)

Source: Computed from DGCIS

of trade improved, whereas the quantity of imports increased relatively rapidly such that the Qx/Qm ratio declined. The impact of these changes has been an increase in the trade deficit with China. The increase in quantity of imports was the result of increase in imports of machinery, chemicals, and fertiliser. All three are major items of import and also commodities for which India depends largely on China. The expansion in imports of these items resulted in a larger deficit with China, as is shown in Figure 4.17.

The increase in the price of exports observed for 2008 was on account of the increase in the unit value of exports for gems and jewellery. While Px/Pm has increased, Qx/Qm has declined over time, primarily because of a faster increase in imports. Such price-quantity movements would suggest that over time, some quantity adjustment may be observed for China.[25] As was shown in Table 4.3, depreciation leads to an increase in exports as well as imports. Unlike the trade with other partners, where commodity

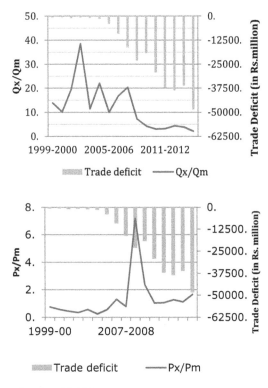

Figure 4.17 Terms of trade with China

Source: Computed from DGCIS

composition can explain the impact of the exchange rate, the estimated relationship for China may have other explanations. The commodity composition consists of commodities that show weak or no response to the exchange rate. For example, copper and cotton contribute a significant proportion of exports to China. While India's share in China's imports for these commodities has been increasing, India competes with countries such as the USA and Chile in market for cotton and copper respectively. Therefore, the fact that India still forms a small share of China's trade, and has to compete in products that do not form a large share of India's exports, makes the exchange rate an important determinant for trade with China.[26]

The imports, on the other hand, consist of machinery, fertilisers, and chemicals. For all these commodities, China has become a major source of imports, and with the increased reliance on these imports for production, it is expected that for these imports there is an expansion with depreciation. Estimated coefficient for imports show a similar result.

Conclusion

Analysis of the bilateral trade with India brings out some important features, such as changes in the countries that are top trading partners as well as changes in the product composition of exports[27] to these trading partners. Over the period 1995 to 2014, the share of the EU countries and the USA declined, whereas that of countries such as China and UAE increased substantially. In terms of product composition, although there has been an increase in product diversification over time for many countries, labour intensive products still dominate exports to some of the major trading partners such as the USA, the UK, and UAE.

One major conclusion that can be drawn in this chapter is that the response of bilateral exports and imports to changes in the exchange rate is determined by product composition. To illustrate, the exchange rate changes have an impact on the changes in exports for the UK, the USA, UAE, Belgium, and Hong Kong. For all these countries, exports consist predominantly of labour intensive products such as textiles and gems and jewellery. The exports of these commodities are known to be more sensitive to price changes owing to competition from countries such as Bangladesh and China. The latter has recently reported a decline in margins charged for polishing of diamonds – one of India's largest traditional markets. In addition to the labour intensive goods, exports to these countries consist of commodities such as pharmaceuticals and machinery. For these commodities, it is shown that Indian exports face stiff price competition and are sensitive to changes in the exchange rate.

On the other hand, countries such as Germany, Japan, Singapore, and the Netherlands, for which changes in the exchange rate were found to have no impact on exports, are countries for which there has been growing product diversification in favour of commodities such as cereals, petroleum products, chemicals, and vehicles (parts thereof). The lack of response to changes in the exchange rate was observed for each of these commodities for separate reasons. For example, exports of vehicles parts and chemicals are linked to global production. Export of rice is influenced by domestic policy on price and exports. Lastly, export of petroleum products is driven by perverse domestic incentives.

In the case of Singapore, when the petroleum products are excluded from exports, the exchange rate turns significant. The non-oil exports consist of commodities that are sensitive to changes in the exchange rate such as machinery, gems and jewellery, and ships, boats, and floating structures.

China is unique in that exports are influenced by factors other than product composition. Even though primary and mineral items dominate exports, exports are sensitive to changes in the exchange rate. One possible explanation for this result is that for exports of these commodities to China, the relative prices matter even though the overall exports may be driven by other factors. Thus, the price of export of these goods to China is evaluated against prices for all other countries after there has been a change in the exchange rate.

Imports are shown to be inelastic to changes in the exchange rate for countries such as Hong Kong, Switzerland, Belgium, the UK, and China. That is, exchange rate depreciation leads to higher value of imports. In the cases of the UK and China, product composition explains this result. Imports from these countries consist of products such as machinery and fertilisers, for which it is shown that import dependence results in such inelasticity. In the cases of Hong Kong, Belgium, and Switzerland, imports are concentrated in a particular item, such as gold or precious stones, within the gems and jewellery segment. The high degree of concentration results in the observed inelasticity of imports.

The multiplier approach to balance of payments posits a positive relationship between income and imports. In the equation for exports and imports, the GDP of the trading partner and domestic GDP were introduced respectively. From the results, it is evident that changes in domestic and foreign income have a positive impact on imports and exports respectively. That is, with an increase in income of the trading partner, the value of bilateral exports increases. Similarly, with an increase in domestic income, imports rise.

Appendix

Table 4A.1 Share of India in imports of trading partners

Country	Indicator	1995	2000	2005	2010	2014
Bangladesh	Share in India's exports	3.14	2.02	1.69	1.36	2.07
	Share of India in imports	15.3	10.5	14	13.9	14.8
Belgium	Share in India's exports	0.00	3.39	2.83	2.26	1.85
	Share of India in imports	–	0.91	0.96	1.25	1.20
Brazil	Share in India's exports	0.32	0.48	1.01	1.65	2.19
	Share of India in imports	0.34	0.61	1.63	2.34	2.90
China, PR: Hong Kong	Share in India's exports	5.96	6.12	4.35	4.27	4.25
	Share of India in imports	0.97	1.29	1.53	2.14	2.28
China, PR: Mainland	Share in India's exports	0.93	1.78	6.59	7.86	4.17
	Share of India in imports	0.30	0.60	1.48	1.50	0.84
France	Share in India's exports	2.24	2.34	2.03	2.20	1.60
	Share of India in imports	0.40	0.35	0.45	0.78	0.86
Germany	Share in India's exports	6.03	4.38	3.46	2.69	2.44
	Share of India in imports	0.57	0.45	0.50	0.69	0.66
Indonesia	Share in India's exports	1.64	0.91	1.39	2.05	1.40
	Share of India in imports	1.18	1.57	1.82	2.43	2.22
Iran, Islamic Republic of	Share in India's exports	0.52	0.49	1.22	1.13	1.39
	Share of India in imports	1.80	1.77	2.60	2.67	5.03
Israel	Share in India's exports	0.60	1.12	1.17	1.26	1.13
	Share of India in imports	0.67	1.45	2.84	3.12	3.10
Italy	Share in India's exports	3.19	2.96	2.51	1.88	1.69
	Share of India in imports	0.65	0.64	0.71	1.04	1.17
Japan	Share in India's exports	6.98	4.15	2.44	2.16	1.80
	Share of India in imports	0.87	0.69	0.62	0.82	0.86
Kenya	Share in India's exports	0.76	0.32	0.55	0.90	1.41
	Share of India in imports	7.90	4.09	8.64	10.93	16.37
Korea, Republic of	Share in India's exports	1.29	1.07	1.66	1.63	1.48
	Share of India in imports	0.59	0.61	0.81	1.33	1.00

(Continued)

Country	Indicator	1995	2000	2005	2010	2014
Malaysia	Share in India's exports	1.16	1.33	1.16	1.59	1.45
	Share of India in imports	0.71	0.88	0.97	1.51	1.95
Nepal	Share in India's exports	0.35	0.34	0.85	0.86	1.39
	Share of India in imports	15.36	36.57	59.45	57.01	56.92
Netherlands	Share in India's exports	2.33	2.07	2.30	2.95	2.12
	Share of India in imports	0.44	0.40	0.54	0.96	0.70
Saudi Arabia	Share in India's exports	1.39	1.88	1.74	2.02	4.03
	Share of India in imports	1.86	2.73	3.09	4.55	8.00
Singapore	Share in India's exports	2.64	1.94	5.16	4.08	3.04
	Share of India in imports	0.74	0.80	2.04	2.97	2.26
South Africa	Share in India's exports	0.88	0.71	1.42	1.63	1.77
	Share of India in imports		0.95	2.03	3.44	4.57
Spain	Share in India's exports	1.25	1.50	1.61	1.04	0.99
	Share of India in imports	0.42	0.47	0.62	0.93	0.90
Sri Lanka	Share in India's exports	1.26	1.42	1.91	1.49	2.02
	Share of India in imports	10.47	8.97	20.71	19.96	20.70
Tanzania	Share in India's exports	0.23	0.23	0.23	0.50	1.09
	Share of India in imports	4.14	5.84	6.99	15.20	24.40
Thailand	Share in India's exports	1.51	1.20	1.05	0.96	1.10
	Share of India in imports	0.82	1.00	1.08	1.23	1.34
Turkey	Share in India's exports	0.51	0.70	0.96	1.04	1.75
	Share of India in imports	0.62	0.82	1.10	1.84	2.85
United Arab Emirates	Share in India's exports	4.28	5.79	8.43	13.24	10.44
	Share of India in imports	6.15	6.60	8.43	17.77	13.33
United Kingdom	Share in India's exports	6.16	5.24	4.80	2.88	3.05
	Share of India in imports	0.86	0.77	0.97	1.36	1.43
United States	Share in India's exports	17.37	21.31	16.78	10.59	13.37
	Share of India in imports	0.79	0.89	1.15	1.56	1.93
Vietnam	Share in India's exports	0.32	0.49	0.67	1.11	2.05
	Share of India in imports	0.74	1.14	1.62	2.11	2.17

Source: DoTS, IMF

Table 4A.2 Estimated equation for exchange rate and trade

Country	Independent variables	Estimated coefficient	
		Log(exports)	*Log(imports)*
Belgium	Log REER	−0.9*(0.56)	−2.54***(0.61)
	Log RER		
	Log GDP of trading partner	6.84***(0.32)	
	Log GDP of India		1.81***(0.08)
	Constant	−173.7***(9.4)	−32.7***(3.6)
	R square	0.96	0.95
China	Log REER	−5.08**(2.18)	−6.46***(2.35)
	Log RER		
	Log GDP of trading partner	3.12***(0.14)	5.26***(0.36)
	Log GDP of India		
	Constant	−60.4***(10.45)	−51.66***(3.45)
	R square	0.95	0.95
Germany	Log REER	−0.004(0.55)	−0.25(0.49)
	Log RER		
	Log GDP of trading partner	8.18***(0.379)	
	Log GDP of India		2.12***(0.07)
	Constant	−229.8***(11.87)	−51.67***(3.45)
	R square	0.937	0.97
Hong Kong	Log REER	−2.37***(0.75)	−2.2***(0.718)
	Log RER		
	Log GDP of trading partner	4.21***(0.18)	
	Log GDP of India		3.52***(0.122)
	Constant	−93.05***(7.16)	−82.2***(4.93)
	R square	0.97	0.97
Japan	Log REER	0.037(0.747)	−0.65(0.41)
	Log RER		
	Log GDP of trading partner	9.5***(1.11)	
	Log GDP of India		1.91***(0.07)
	Constant	−272.2***(34.18)	−44.2***(3.15)
	R square	0.8	0.97
Netherlands	Log REER	0.533(1.28)	−0.36(0.44)
	Log RER		
	Log GDP of trading partner	7.49***(0.55)	
	Log GDP of India		2.01***(0.07)
	Constant	−201.7***(18.26)	−49.7***(3.31)
	R square	0.87	0.96

(Continued)

Table 4A.2 (Continued)

Country	Independent variables	Estimated coefficient	
		Log(exports)	*Log(imports)*
Saudi Arabia	Log REER	1(1.48)	0.97(1.62)
	Log RER		
	Log GDP of trading partner	3.85***(0.21)	
	Log GDP of India		2.855***(0.24)
	Constant	−102.1***(7.12)	−77.34***(11.87)
	R square	0.968	0.71
Singapore	Log REER	0.66(1.18)	−0.66(0.62)
	Log RER		
	Log GDP of trading partner	3.47***(0.146)	
	Log GDP of India		2.42***(0.09)
	Constant	−86.8***(8.43)	−75.1***(8.68)
	R square	0.95	0.97
Switzerland	Log REER		−4.15***(1.23)
	Log RER		
	Log GDP of trading partner		
	Log GDP of India		3.63***(0.22)
	Constant		−75.1***(8.68)
	R square		0.94
UAE	Log REER	−2.64***(0.76)	0.1(0.87)
	Log RER		
	Log GDP of trading partner	4.81***(0.19)	
	Log GDP of India		3.19***(0.16)
	Constant	−106.17***(6.17)	−82.45***(6.28)
	R square	0.97	0.89
UK	Log REER	−0.95**(0.39)	−1.83***(0.54)
	Log RER		
	Log GDP of trading partner	5.25***(0.7)	
	Log GDP of India		1.57***(0.08)
	Constant	−139.6***(19.9)	−29.73***(3.38)
	R square	0.93	0.95
USA	Log REER	−1.42*(0.74)	0.013(0.45)
	Log RER		
	Log GDP of trading partner	5.33***(0.26)	
	Log GDP of India		2.29***(0.06)
	constant	−147.7***(9.45)	−56.95***(3.21)
		0.96	0.97

Note: * means significant at 10%, ** means significant at 5%, and *** means significant at 1%

Source: Estimated

Table 4A.3 Impact of exchange rate on non-oil exports to Singapore

Variables	Log(non-oil exports to Singapore)
Log REER	−0.07*
Log GDP	0.012**
Constant	−0.59
R square	0.33

Note: * means significant at 10%, ** means significant at 5%, and *** means significant at 1%

Source: Estimated

Table 4A.4 Commodity-wise (HS two-digit) exports

	UK			
Commodity	*2000*	*Share*	*2014*	*Share*
Articles of apparel not knitted or crocheted	123,692	11.8	584,434	10.3
Footwear	71,782	6.8	303,945	5.3
Gems and jewellery	68,005	6.5	311,171	5.5
Articles of apparel knitted or crocheted	61,611	5.9	551,853	9.7
Articles of leather	53,413	5.1	183,625	3.2
Other made up textile articles	48,357	4.6	181,611	3.2
Non-electrical machinery	47,008	4.5	455,666	8.0
Electrical machinery	37,330	3.6	255,295	4.5
Cotton	36,221	3.4	18,727	0.3
Coffee, tea, mate, and spices	32,249	3.1	77,807	1.4
Articles of iron and steel	31,621	3.0	228,025	4.0
Cereals	30,753	2.9	97,374	1.7
Organic chemicals	28,480	2.7	149,287	2.6
Fish and crustaceans	27,821	2.6	92,965	1.6
Vehicles and parts thereof	25,903	2.5	336,823	5.9
	Japan			
Commodity	*2000*	*Share*	*2014*	*Share*
Fish and crustaceans	231,204	28.2	263,817	8.0
Gems and jewellery	176,524	21.5	172,910	5.3
Ores, slag, and ash	60,924	7.4	132,609	4.0
Articles of apparel not knitted or crocheted	45,388	5.5	103,426	3.1

(Continued)

Table 4A.4 (Continued)

Japan				
Commodity	2000	Share	2014	Share
Cotton	33,725	4.1	39,770	1.2
Organic chemicals	20,071	2.4	210,568	6.4
Other made up textile articles	19,834	2.4	34,707	1.1
Iron and steel	17,729	2.2	149,806	4.6
Residues and waste from food industry	15,631	1.9	26,680	0.8
Coffee, tea, mate, and spices	14,781	1.8	26,556	0.8
Edible fruit and nuts	12,810	1.6	36,486	1.1
Petroleum products	3,783	0.5	1,124,767	34.3

Germany				
Commodity	2000	Share	2014	Share
Articles of apparel not knitted or crocheted	101,380	11.6	351,543	7.6
Articles of leather	89,285	10.2	253,395	5.5
Articles of apparel knitted or crocheted	61,086	7.0	394,515	8.6
Carpets and other floor coverings	55,101	6.3	82,939	1.8
Organic chemicals	51,572	5.9	365,441	7.9
Footwear	45,296	5.2	233,097	5.1
Other made up textile articles	44,592	5.1	177,020	3.8
Non-electrical machinery	43,719	5.0	367,009	8.0
Gems and jewellery	35,561	4.1	69,679	1.5
Coffee, tea, mate, and spices	27,103	3.1	84,476	1.8
Electrical machinery	26,214	3.0	267,853	5.8
Miscellaneous goods	23,436	2.7	7,308	0.2
Cotton	20,739	2.4	53,546	1.2
Vehicle and parts thereof	16,132	1.9	183,629	4.0

Singapore				
Commodity	2000	Share	2014	Share
Gems and jewellery	55,510	13.9	301,502	5.0
Electrical machinery	52,323	13.1	137,865	2.3
Aluminium and articles made thereof	37,691	9.4	13,261	0.2
Residues and waste from food industry	34,679	8.7	3,443	0.1
Organic chemicals	21,555	5.4	169,331	2.8
Non-electrical machinery	21,089	5.3	260,291	4.3
Cotton	12,012	3.0	3,326	0.1
Articles of apparel not knitted or crocheted	11,969	3.0	25,130	0.4
Miscellaneous goods	9,189	2.3	26,202	0.4
Iron and steel	8,657	2.2	9,752	0.2
Fish and crustaceans	7,960	2.0	26,441	0.4

	Singapore			
Commodity	2000	Share	2014	Share
Articles of iron and steel	7,788	1.9	35,245	0.6
Tanning or dyeing extracts	6,730	1.7	38,013	0.6
Plastics and articles thereof	6,646	1.7	20,435	0.3
Petroleum products	23	0	3,253,686	54.4

	UAE			
Commodity	2000	Share	2014	Share
Gems and jewellery	202,650	17.1	7,514,356	37.2
Articles of apparel not knitted or crocheted	192,685	16.2	921,355	4.6
Articles of apparel knitted or crocheted	56,042	4.7	700,127	3.5
Articles of iron and steel	52,203	4.4	428,191	2.1
Man-made filaments	47,181	4.0	170,375	0.8
Cotton	41,660	3.5	86,886	0.4
Coffee, tea, mate and spices	38,787	3.3	99,155	0.5
Iron and steel	33,042	2.8	391,951	1.9
Fish and crustaceans	32,449	2.7	104,757	0.5
Non-electrical machinery	29,989	2.5	434,551	2.2
Electrical machinery	29,178	2.5	376,670	1.9

	USA			
Commodity	2000	Share	2014	Share
Gems and jewellery	1,252,780	29.5	5,146,674	19.8
Articles of apparel not knitted or crocheted	628,760	14.8	1,221,323	4.7
Articles of apparel knitted or crocheted	214,802	5.1	991,020	3.8
Other made up articles of textile	191,619	4.5	1,354,066	5.2
Miscellaneous goods	158,360	3.7	36,200	0.1
Articles of iron and steel	137,525	3.2	1,048,169	4.0
Carpets and other floor coverings	133,958	3.2	469,220	1.8
Articles of leather	109,110	2.6	271,932	1.0
Fish and crustaceans	108,333	2.5	849,399	3.3
Non-electrical machinery	104,884	2.5	1,320,566	5.1
Iron and steel	101,979	2.4	428,056	1.7
Organic chemicals	101,358	2.4	1,002,020	3.9
Electrical machinery	97,018	2.3	773,744	3.0
Edible fruits	94,580	2.2	150,244	0.6
Vehicle and parts thereof	55,001	1.3	787,999	3.0
Cotton	54,217	1.3	55,475	0.2
Petroleum products	720	0	2,362,869	9.1
Pharmaceutical products	25,664	0.6	2,302,005	8.9

(Continued)

	China			
Commodity	*2000*	*Share*	*2014*	*Share*
Ores, slag, and ash	70,958	18.7	311,652	4.3
Fish and crustaceans	52,895	13.9	72,599	1.0
Organic chemicals	49,383	13.0	640,147	8.8
Plastics and articles thereof	36,990	9.7	217,350	3.0
Cotton	32,167	8.5	1,395,943	19.1
Salt, sulphur, etc.	21,908	5.8	379,960	5.2
Iron and Steel	12,512	3.3	72,196	1.0
Pharmaceutical products	8,236	2.2	18,140	0.2
Prepared feathers and articles thereof	8,117	2.1	100,092	1.4
Non-electrical machinery	8,023	2.1	305,505	4.2
Copper and articles thereof	7,097	1.9	1,156,291	15.8
Electrical machinery	6,451	1.7	171,224	2.3
Articles of stone, cement, etc.	6,375	1.7	13,299	0.2
Petroleum products	387	0.1	787,995	10.8

	Hong Kong			
Commodity	*2000*	*Share*	*2014*	*Share*
Gems and jewellery	797,409	66.1	7,460,577	89.8
Cotton	93,479	7.7	56,324	0.7
electrical machinery	73,561	6.1	133,891	1.6
Raw hides and skin	41,348	3.4	242,839	2.9
Organic chemicals	40,895	3.4	22,429	0.3
Pharmaceutical products	15,111	1.3	12,620	0.2
Articles of apparel not knitted or crocheted	12,120	1.0	29,067	0.3
Tanning or dyeing extracts	11,275	0.9	11,103	0.1
Plastics and articles thereof	10,140	0.8	12,395	0.1
Iron and steel	9,973	0.8	5,495	0.1
Fish and crustaceans	8,390	0.7	59,967	0.7

	Saudi Arabia			
Commodity	*2000*	*Share*	*2014*	*Share*
Cereals	131,335	34.9	794,519	11.7
Articles of apparel not knitted or crocheted	38,609	10.3	105,277	1.5
Edible fruit and nuts	15,434	4.1	80,561	1.2
Articles of apparel knitted or crocheted	11,897	3.2	77,896	1.1
Articles of iron and steel	9,235	2.5	373,045	5.5
Non-electrical machinery	9,234	2.5	232,110	3.4
Coffee, tea, mate, and spices	8,767	2.3	65,271	1
Man-made filaments	8,729	2.3	10,873	0.2

Saudi Arabia				
Commodity	2000	Share	2014	Share
Man-made staple fibres	8,384	2.2	12,543	0.2
Iron and steel	8,254	2.2	142,146	2.1
Copper and articles thereof	8,088	2.2	36,158	0.5
Electrical machinery	7,741	2.1	153,356	2.3
Organic chemicals	7,651	2	164,900	2.4
Petroleum products	58	0	3,383,627	49.7

Netherlands				
Commodity	2000	Share	2014	Share
Edible fruits and nuts	42,516	10.6	93,625	2.4
Articles of apparel not knitted or crocheted	41,266	10.3	140,436	3.6
Articles of apparel knitted or crocheted	31,043	7.7	126,049	3.3
Organic chemicals	25,301	6.3	240,604	6.2
Misc. chemical products	17,683	4.4	65,196	1.7
Articles of leather	17,265	4.3	68,166	1.8
Electrical machinery	16,833	4.2	194,909	5.0
Miscellaneous goods	14,860	3.7	397	0
Animal or vegetable fats	13,963	3.5	78,379	2.0
Non-electrical machinery	13,115	3.3	81,326	2.1
Other articles made of textile	11,467	2.9	69,025	1.8
Pharmaceutical products	10,854	2.7	102,552	2.7
Vehicles and parts thereof	9,897	2.5	118,265	3.1
Petroleum products	649	0.2	1,508,872	39.0

Belgium				
Commodity	2000	Share	2014	Share
Gems and jewellery	415,376	61.8	1,636,241	48.5
Cotton	23,924	3.6	24,342	0.7
Articles of apparel not knitted or crocheted	21,662	3.2	67,254	2.0
Other vegetable textile fibres	15,264	2.3	5,942	0.2
Other made up textile articles	12,822	1.9	42,888	1.3
Organic chemicals	12,819	1.9	260,704	7.7
Man-made staple fibres	10,959	1.6	37,747	1.1
Articles of apparel knitted or crocheted	10,558	1.6	87,724	2.6
Electrical machinery	10,110	1.5	39,057	1.2
Iron and steel	9,657.7	1.4	171,512.9	5.1
Fish and crustaceans	8,913.8	1.3	117,478.3	3.5

Note: * means significant at 10%, ** means significant at 5%, and *** means significant at 1%

Source: DGCIS

Table 4A.5 Commodity-wise (HS two-digit) imports

	UK			
Commodity	2000	Share	2014	Share
Gems and jewellery	1,006,889	69.6	708711	23.1
Non-electrical machinery	88,293	6.1	427,685	13.9
Electrical machinery	57,398	4.0	189,459	6.2
Iron and steel	43,918	3.0	294,800	9.6
Optical, photographics, and cinematographic instruments	28,052	1.9	164,533	5.4
Organic chemicals	25,036	1.7	54,522	1.8
Project goods	16,583	1.1	14,203	0.5
Aluminium and articles thereof	7,209	0.5	135,432	4.4
Beverages, spirits, and vinegar	2,350	0.2	131,131	4.3

	USA			
Commodity	2000	Share	2014	Share
Non-electrical machinery	280,977	20.4	1,842,210	13.8
Electrical machinery	209,556	15.2	1,048,703	7.9
Optical, photographic, and cinematographic instruments	105,376	7.7	854,419	6.4
Organic chemicals	82,017	6.0	458,846	3.4
Gems and jewellery	79,205	5.8	2,158,419	16.2
Aircraft, spacecraft, and parts thereof	76,737	5.6	1,423,304	10.7
Pulp of wood	40,905	3.0	357,496	2.7
Plastic and articles thereof	39,508	2.9	507,696	3.8
Misc. chemical products	38,210	2.8	474,164	3.6
Fertilisers	28,896	2.1	186,254	1.4

	UAE			
Commodity	2000	Share	2014	Share
Gems and jewellery	113,531	37.7	5,376,068	33.7
Petroleum products	73,976	24.6	8,238,213	51.6
Salt, sulphur, etc.	21,399	7.1	192,177	1.2
Iron and steel	14,784	4.9	349,697	2.2
Aluminium and articles thereof	9,208	3.1	306,759	1.9
Organic chemicals	7,403	2.5	6,930	0
Copper and articles thereof	6,992	2.3	390,451	2.4
Non-electrical machinery	5,712	1.9	57,764	0.4

	Japan			
Commodity	2000	Share	2014	Share
Non-electrical machinery	219,922	26.1	1,508,436	24.3
Electrical machinery	100,624	12.0	587,034	9.5
Vehicles and parts thereof	72,244	8.6	337,354	5.4
Optical, photographic, and cinematographic instruments	58,089	6.9	333,268	5.4
Organic chemicals	55,672	6.6	252,489	4.1
Iron and steel	45,055	5.4	890,427	14.4
Project goods	35,661	4.2	176,468	2.8
Photographic and cinematographic goods	33,213	3.9	25,636	0.4
Rubber and articles thereof	32,119	3.8	160,636	2.6
Articles of iron and steel	30,796	3.7	242,647	3.9
Plastics and articles thereof	27,879	3.3	270,853	4.4

	Hong Kong			
Commodity	2000	Share	2014	Share
Gems and jewellery	225,236	57.9	2,504,646	73.5
Non-electrical machinery	45,950	11.8	110,505	3.2
Electrical machinery	43,364	11.1	407,397	12.0

	Germany			
Commodity	2000	Share	2014	Share
Non-electrical machinery	244,026	30.4	2,187,510	28.0
electrical machinery	101,262	12.6	860,248	11.0
Optical, photographic, and cinematographic instruments	65,407	8.1	590,173	7.5
Organic chemicals	53,532	6.7	443,335	5.7
Project goods	41,533	5.2	260,655	3.3
Plastics and articles thereof	31,611	3.9	415,966	5.3
Iron and steel	31,019	3.9	194,712	2.5

	Singapore			
Commodity	2000	Share	2014	Share
Non-electrical machinery	217,138	32.5	668,539	15.4
Electrical machinery	158,373	23.7	555,135	12.7
Organic chemicals	51,820	7.7	871,583	20.0
Printed book, newspapers	34,265	5.1	13,671	0.3
Optical, photographic, and cinematographic instruments	26,728	4.0	207,370	4.8
Gems and jewellery	19,023	2.8	190,147	4.4
Plastics and articles thereof	18,156	2.7	510,834	11.7
Ships, boats, and floating structures	15,443	2.3	152,720	3.5
Iron and steel	10,787	1.6	138,531	3.2

(Continued)

Table 4A.5 (Continued)

	China			
Commodity	2000	Share	2014	Share
Petroleum products	120,271	17.5	474,808	1.3
Organic chemicals	113,884	16.6	3,863,625	10.5
Non-electrical machinery	86,193	12.6	6,208,193	16.8
Electrical machinery	73,757	10.7	10,236,143	27.7
Silk	51,778	7.5	122,253	0.3
Fertilisers	3,873	0.6	1,937,526	5.2
Iron and steel	4,526	0.7	1,663,061	4.5

	Saudi Arabia			
Commodity	2000	Share	2014	Share
Petroleum products	122,005	43	14,134,476	82.6
Organic chemicals	60,019	21.2	772,179	4.5
Inorganic chemicals	52,453	18.5	180,560	1.1
Plastics and articles thereof	13,469	4.7	693,677	4.1
Salt, sulphur, etc.	9,725	3.4	55,682	0.3

	Belgium			
Commodity	2000	Share	2014	Share
Gems and jewellery	1,176,150	89.7	5,499,154	83.4
Non-electrical machinery	24,979	1.9	183,248	2.8
Plastics and articles thereof	9,281	0.7	162,608	2.5
Iron and steel	13,400	1.0	106,235	1.6
Organic chemicals	11,805	0.9	87,142	1.3

	Netherlands			
Commodity	2000	Share	2014	Share
Ships, boats, and floating structures	36,366	18.2	48,196	2.8
Organic chemicals	31,034	15.5	123,081	7.2
Non-electrical machinery	19,873	9.9	178,943	10.5
Optical, photographic, and cinematographic instruments	15,749	7.9	60,756	3.6
Electrical machinery	13,402	6.7	72,199	4.2
Pulp of wood	9,402	4.7	8,545	0.5
Plastics and articles thereof	8,835	4.4	171,321	10.0
Project goods	8,612	4.3	5,276	0.3
Paper and paperboards	7,361	3.7	43,275	2.5
Iron and steel	6,952	3.5	119,111	7.0
Petroleum products	0	0	463,198	27.1

Source: DGCIS

Table 4A.6 Regression for SITC three-digit classification

Commodity name	Log REER	Log GDP	Constant	Share in category
Textile yarn	2.8	1.3	−5.4	2.0
Cotton fabrics, woven	1.6	0.5	0.4	0.6
Fabrics, woven, of man-made fabrics	−2.5	1.7	3.2	0.7
Other textile fabrics, woven	−1.3	0.2	7.1	0.1
Knitted or crocheted fabrics	−0.7	2.6	−6.0	0.1
Tulles, trimmings, lace, ribbons	1.1	1.5	−4.2	0.1
Special yarn, special textile fabric	1.7	2.2	−8.2	0.2
Made up articles, of textile materials	1.5	1.4	−3.4	1.4
Floor coverings, etc.	2.0	1.0	−2.9	0.6
Nails, screws, nuts, bolts, rivets	2.3	2.4	−10.6	0.3
Internal combustion piston engines	0.9	2.8	−9.3	0.7
Telecommunication equipment, NES	−9.0	5.0	0.1	0.5
Electrical machinery and apparatus	−0.5	2.1	−3.0	0.4
Motor vehicles for the transport of persons	−2.7	4.6	−10.3	1.8
Parts and accessories of vehicles	2.6	2.7	−12.0	1.4
Aircraft and associated equipment	−3.6	5.4	−12.7	2.1
Ships, boats, and floating structures	−6.3	6.0	−9.7	1.4
Travel goods, handbags, and similar articles	0.8	1.4	−2.5	0.4
Men's clothing of textile fabrics, not knitted or crocheted	0.9	0.7	1.0	0.8
Women's clothing, of textile fabrics	−0.3	1.0	2.2	1.4
Men's or boy's clothing, of knitted or crocheted	−0.1	0.9	2.0	0.5
Women's clothing, of textile, knitted	−1.7	1.6	1.9	0.5
Articles of apparel, of textile NES	0.6	1.8	−3.4	1.8
Clothing accessories, of textile	−1.4	1.8	0.0	0.4
Articles of apparel, clothing accessories	0.2	1.1	0.3	0.3
Footwear	1.0	1.6	−3.4	0.9
Fish and crustaceans	2.7	1.1	−4.2	3.0
Hydrocarbons, NES, and halogenated, nitr. derivative	1.0	3.8	−13.8	0.8
Alcohols, phenols, halogenat., sulfonat., nitrat. der.	3.1	2.4	−12.0	0.4
Carboxylic acids, anhydrides, halides, per.; derivati.	2.2	2.3	−9.5	0.4
Nitrogen-function compounds	0.8	1.9	−4.8	0.5
Organo-inorganic, heterocycl. compounds, nucl. acids	1.4	3.0	−11.2	0.8
Other organic chemicals	−1.1	2.6	−3.7	0.7
Copper and articles of copper	2.0	2.5	−12.5	0.0
Leather products	0.7	1.0	−2.9	0.8
Ores, slag, and ash	−3.8	2.4	−0.4	0.0

Note: * means significant at 10%, ** means significant at 5%, and *** means significant at 1%

Source: Estimated

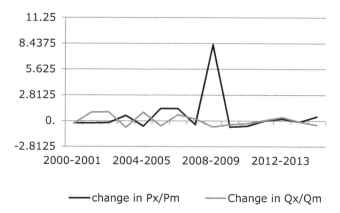

Figure 4A.1 Changes in Px/Pm and Qx/Qm for China

Source: Computed from DGCIS

Notes

1 Note that while annual estimates have been reported here, the same equations were estimated using quarterly data using the VAR model. It is important to point out that the results do not change, since it is found that the adjustment process for all countries takes up to four quarters, i.e. a year.
2 The coefficient for Saudi Arabia is estimated from 1999 to 2014, since the year 2000 marks a structural shift in trade with Saudi Arabia. The export of petroleum products went from 0.01 per cent in the period prior to 1999 to 2 per cent in 2002, after which the share of petroleum expanded. In fact, the growth in exports was largely because of growth in exports of petroleum products. Following 2000, the total value of exports and the share of petroleum in exports increased manifold. In order to take care of this break, the years prior to 1999 were dropped.
3 Commodity-wise (HS two-digit) exports and imports are given in Table 4A.4 and Table 4A.5, respectively.
4 "The Future of India-Saudi Arabia Relations," April 2016.
5 This includes articles of apparel knitted and crocheted as well as not knitted and crocheted (HS codes 61 and 62).
6 The top ten items other than gems and jewellery, and petroleum products, accounted for 27 per cent of exports in 2014.
7 The crude price levels (Brent) in 2011 were $111.26/barrel.
8 Para 21, Government of India (2015).
9 "Diamond exporters fear losing market to HK, Bangkok", March 2013.
10 For these items check the Appendix, Table 4A.6.
11 "Silver exports help UK trade deficit narrow in October", December 2014.
12 Check the Appendix, Table 4A.6, for results on carpets and footwear.
13 For example, among the top 15 exports, the commodities that are shown to respond to exchange rate comprise 32 per cent, whereas those that do not are 28 per cent.
14 "Japanese seafood exports rising as nation eats less fish," September 2015.
15 "Will the 'India boom' shake Japan?" March 2014.

16 "Gems, jewellery exports dip 5.30% in FY16 on weak international demand," April 2016.
17 "Six countries including China, Japan and Russia dump steel in India: DGAD," April 2016.
18 For this purpose, the detailed analysis of imports has not been undertaken.
19 "Mining to come to a halt in Goa, government to scrutinize documents," September 2011.
20 "China looks for alternatives as India's iron ore exports fall."
21 "China reopens door to Indian marine exports," June 2012.
22 "Modi's 'Make in India' push to depend on Chinese steel," November 2014.
23 "Rising silk yarn output helps cut imports from China," November 2013.
24 "Met coke producers alarmed over cheaper Chinese imports," December 2014.
25 Note that that throughout the period the price and quantity have moved in opposite directions (see the Appendix, Figure 4A.1). The observation in 2009 does not allow us to observe this; therefore, the graph for changes brings out the movements better. However, after 2011, the relationship may have weakened due to global slowdown in demand. Therefore, except for three years, this result is observed; which is why the coefficient for exchange rate is negative and significant for exports.
26 Using the bilateral exchange rate in place of the effective exchange rate gave similar results except in the case of China. The fact that bilateral exchange rate does not matter means that China's decision to import from India depends on the value of the rupee expressed in relation to other currencies.
27 A more disaggregate analysis of commodities was taken to find that the results of two-digit disaggregation suffice to explain the direction of impact. The regressions for various important sub-categories are reported in Table 4A.6 and show that the sign of the coefficient for major sub-categories is the same as that for the two-digit classification.

References

Bhattacharya, S.K. and Bhattacharya, B.N., 2006. Free trade agreement between People's Republic of China and India: Likely impact and its implications to Asian economic community (No. 59). ADB Institute Discussion Papers.

"China looks for alternatives as India's iron ore exports fall" available at http://maritimegateway.com/mgw/index.php/news/exim-news/534-china-looks-for-alternatives-as-indias-iron-ore-exports-fall

"China reopens door to Indian marine exports", June 2012 available at www.foodnavigator-asia.com/Markets/China-reopens-doors-to-Indian-marine-exports

"Diamond exporters fear losing market to HK, Bangkok," March 2013 available at www.business-standard.com/article/economy-policy/diamond-exporters-fear-losing-market-to-hk-bangkok-113030100531_1.html

Government of India, 2015. "External Affairs Minister's Statement at the 11th India-UAE Joint Commission Meeting in New Delhi", September 3, 2015, available at http://www.mea.gov.in/Speeches-Statements.htm?dtl/25785/External_Affairs_Ministers_Statement_at_the_11th_IndiaUAE_Joint_Commission_Meeting_in_New_Delhi__September_3_2015

"Japanese seafood exports rising as nation eats less fish," September 2015 available at www.bloomberg.com/news/articles/2015-09-14/sushi-losing-to-meat-means-japan-flying-fish-surplus-across-asia

"Met coke producers alarmed over cheaper Chinese imports," December 2014 available at www.thehindubusinessline.com/economy/macro-economy/met-coke-makers-raiseconcern-on-cheaper-imports/article6651908.ece

Mukherjee, S. and Mukherjee, S., 2012. *Overview of India' export performance: Trends and drivers.*

Palit, A., 2008. *India-Singapore trade relations.* Institute of South Asian Studies.

"Rising silk yarn output helps cut imports from China," November 2013 available at www.thehindu.com/business/Industry/rising-silk-yarn-output-helps-cut-imports-from-china/article5368449.ece

"Silver exports help UK trade deficit narrow in October," December 2014 available at www.telegraph.co.uk/finance/economics/11284508/Silver-exports-help-UK-trade-deficit-narrow-in-October.html

"The future of India-Saudi Arabia relations," April 2016 available at http://thediplomat.com/2016/04/the-future-of-india-saudi-arabia-relations/

"Will the 'India boom' shake Japan?" March 2014 available at www.eastasiaforum.org/2014/03/05/will-the-india-boom-shake-japan/

Chapter 5

Conclusion

The purpose of this book was to present systematic evidence for India that allows an economist and a policy maker to be able to conclusively say that the exchange rate has significant influence on merchandise trade or otherwise. The elaborate empirical results presented in various chapters make a compelling case that, indeed, the nature of commodities that India trades drives such impact. For example, if the basket of exports consists largely of labour intensive goods, then an exchange rate depreciation would certainly mean higher exports. This is also true in the case of bilateral exports that consist predominantly of labour intensive commodities. While this is the crux of the results, many more striking features of India's trade emerged in the analysis. It is important that the key takeaways from such incidental discussions are not lost, especially since these features are bound to influence any trade strategy.

Changes in product composition and direction of trade

As has been shown, the structure of India's trade has transformed over the period 2000 to 2014. Exports, which earlier comprised mostly labour intensive products, are now being replaced by a larger share of capital intensive manufactures. While such a shift has been observed in composition, there have been some changes in composition that are to the detriment of India's trade. A prime example of such a shift has been stupendous growth in exports of cotton accompanied by sluggish growth in exports of apparel. Further, when revealed comparative advantage (RCA) for India's trade is evaluated, commodities such as meat, rice, and cotton have made significant gains in RCA with relatively high scores. Therefore, despite the increase in the importance of the manufactures in the export basket, the rise of primary commodities as India's RCA is an indication of the fact that India is still preferred for exports of low-value products. However, even among the primary commodities in which India is known to possess a comparative advantage, some exports have been severely affected in recent years. For example, in the case of meat, for which India is known to be the largest exporter, the ban on beef imposed by the incumbent government has dealt a severe blow to exports.

India's direction of trade has also shown marked shifts over the period 2000 to 2014. While there has been a rise in exports to the Middle East and developing Asia, the share of the EU has witnessed a decline. The product disaggregated analysis of bilateral trade suggests similarity of product composition for individual countries within regions. The EU, for example, is the largest market for India's exports of apparel. On the other hand, India's exports of machinery are directed to developing Asia and the Middle East, and India's traditional markets for gems and jewellery continue to be the largest among Middle East countries. Thus, the potential to increase India's exports in manufacturing, and gems and jewellery, can be realised with the expansion of trade with Asia and the Middle East. As for export of apparel, the EU and the USA have remained the traditional markets for these exports. The fact that the share of trade with EU is on a decline will make it difficult to push higher exports of apparel to this region, more so since the EU has recently taken discriminatory action against India's apparel exports. Other countries to which India exports apparel are those in the Middle East, for example UAE and Saudi Arabia. Therefore, given that the Middle East and the USA provide relatively large markets, India can increase its exports of apparel through higher trade with these countries.

The role of China in India's trade cannot be ignored, both as a competitor and as a source of major imports. While China has emerged as a major export destination for India, the categories of products that India exports to China are lower in the value chain as compared to imports from China. Cotton is amongst the top items of export to China and is an important input to the apparel industry. Therefore, the sluggish growth of Indian apparel exports accompanied by a rapid expansion in cotton exports is a discomforting feature. There has been some expansion in the trade of machinery and chemicals; however, the relatively fast expansion of imports has yielded a deficit with China within these categories. To add to the worry, India also competes with China in many segments such as machinery and chemicals (Francis, 2015). Another worrying development in the recent period has been that China has gained significant cost advantage in the polishing of diamonds, which is considered one of India's traditional exports. Therefore, China is a major source of supply of imports of manufactures, while it also competes with Indian exports. Having stated that China has ventured into industries such as apparel and polishing of gems where India possesses a comparative advantage, it is also observed that there has been a decline in the similarity[1] of exports between India and China. Though India competes with China in market for many of its exports, the decline in the similarity of exports can be viewed as a positive development.

In the preceding chapters, empirical evidence was provided for the impact of the exchange rate on trade. From the detailed analysis of disaggregated trade, some important facts emerged about the qualitative changes in product composition as well as the changes in significant trading partners. It was also observed that changes in policies with respect to tariffs and export controls exert a significant influence on trade and often undermine the impact that the exchange rate could have on trade. This chapter, therefore, brings together the results of the preceding chapters to understand the circumstances in which real exchange rate depreciation would result in an improvement in exports and a reduction in imports.

What influences the exchange rate?

As a precursor to the discussion on whether the exchange rate matters in the case of merchandise trade, some important questions were raised about what impacts the exchange rate in India. Two important results emerge from this exercise. One, movements in the exchange rate are determined by changes in expectations that are reflected in movements in the more volatile portfolio flows. Two, the trade deficit is a less significant component of the balance of payments that exercises less influence on the exchange rate.

The discussion in Chapter 2 sheds light on the important role played by the RBI, not just in periods of fixed exchange rates, but also in the period following liberalisation when there was a move to market-determined rates. The Bank's commitment to curb pronounced volatility in the value of the exchange rate has resulted in numerous interventions. In spite of such commitment, volatility has been a feature of the period 1990–2014 due to the growing prominence of portfolio flows in the balance of payments. These flows appear small on a net basis; however, taken as a proportion of inflows and outflows, these account for a substantial part of the balance of payments. Therefore, to ascertain what components of balance of payments have an impact on the exchange rate, a test for causality was undertaken. What emerged from this analysis is that portfolio flows as well as changes in foreign exchange reserves influence movements in the exchange rate. Portfolio flows are a function of various factors such as the state of the economy and global liquidity conditions. For example, during the financial crisis, India experienced a massive surge in capital inflows due to lower returns and increased perceptions of risk in the developed economies. However, in May 2013 when the Federal Reserve put forth the proposal of tapering quantitative easing, India was the worst affected by sharp exchange rate depreciation (Aizeman et al., 2014). Thus, such sharp reversals in flows that are, in turn, determined by the expectations have an impact on the exchange rate.

The results for causality also show that changes in foreign exchange reserves have an impact on the exchange rate.

While it was shown that trade deficit has no causal relationship with the exchange rate, it does not rule out the possible impact of the exchange rate on exports and imports taken separately. Therefore, the equations for imports and exports were estimated separately. However, in order to explain the coefficients for exchange rate for both exports and imports, it was first examined whether domestic prices respond to changes in the exchange rate.

Does the exchange rate impact on domestic prices?

The question raised in the book was whether changes in the exchange rate lead to price changes and whether such price changes, in turn, result in changes in quantities of exports and imports. For this, an estimate of pass through and an analysis of price-quantity changes were provided in Chapter 2. The results presented in this chapter indicate that while domestic prices do not move in response to changes in the exchange rate, the price of tradables is altered by such changes. Note that since price is denominated in local currency, it is expected that exchange rate movement would directly affect price of tradables.

It was seen that the nominal effective exchange rate and the real effective exchange rate tended to move together, and even the introduction of lags did not change this result. This co-movement provided the crudest demonstration of a lack of movement in relative prices. However, in the recent period, i.e. post February 2012, the REER and NEER have moved in opposite directions, primarily due to domestic price movements.

In order to establish whether there are price adjustments in response to changes in the exchange rate, in Chapter 2 exchange rate pass through was estimated. It was found that while some of the variance in domestic prices is explained by the variance in the exchange rate, the relationship between the two is weak (since only 18% of the variation in WPI is explained by NEER).

Having shown that the changes in the exchange rate demonstrate a weak pass through to aggregate domestic prices, the price of only tradables was considered. From the estimated equations, it was seen that the prices of exports and imports measured by their unit values (in rupees) increase with depreciation and decrease with appreciation.

Thus, the monetarist view that a change in the exchange rate must translate into a change in the domestic prices was not upheld by the results, which showed that the pass through to domestic prices is weak or incomplete. Further, since it was shown that the price of tradables responds to changes in the exchange rate, it provides reasonable grounds to examine whether quantities adjust to price changes. To verify if price adjustments lead to quantity adjustment, the correlations between price and quantity changes were presented. It was observed that the response in quantity was weak for exports, whereas the quantity of imports increased with a fall in prices.

Does the exchange rate affect trade?

The central them and principle purpose of this book was to establish whether in India exchange rates play a role at all in influencing merchandise trade. The preliminary results for aggregate analysis were instrumental in the structure of the research in this book. As was clear from the aggregates, the answer perhaps depends on the commodity composition. In pursuit of the answer, a further disaggregate analysis was undertaken. If the key results were to be summarised, it would be as follows.

For the aggregate trade, the exchange rate plays a weak role and, as is demonstrated in the subsequent chapters, the response of all commodities is not similar. In Chapter 3 it was shown that exports of commodities such as gems and jewellery, apparel, machinery, and pharmaceuticals respond to changes in the exchange rate, whereas other major exports seem to be unresponsive (or even change in the opposite direction to the expected one). The commodities where little or no impact was found tend to be subject to the greater influence of domestic policies. Similarly, imports of items such as machinery and fertilisers are inelastic, whereas others do not respond to changes in the exchange rate. Such product composition, in turn, determines countries for which changes in the exchange rate yield a response in exports and imports. For example, exports to the USA, UAE, and Belgium respond to changes in the exchange rate, whereas exports to Saudi Arabia and Germany do not. To lead the discussion onto what policy must or can do, the finer details are described herein.

Aggregate exports and imports

The price and quantity adjustments that have been shown at various points in the book are evidence that make a case for adjustments that ensue an exchange rate adjustment. The exchange rate was observed to have no impact on trade. However, an answer as simple as that merits a discussion of how, since there was evidence of price-quantity movements. The weak response of quantity to changes in prices was corroborated by the regression results for non-oil exports. On the other hand, strong quantity adjustments were demonstrated for imports. As is expected from these results, imports were found to increase with appreciation. On the other hand, oil exports and imports displayed a separate mechanism and direction of adjustment. Changes in the exchange rate were found to have no impact on exports, whereas for imports in the short run (i.e. over a quarter), an expansion was observed following depreciation. In the long run, however, the impact of the exchange rate on oil imports dissipates; a result that is found to hold for the annual estimates provided in Chapters 3 and 4. The lack of response of the oil component of exports is attributable to the wedge that appeared between domestic and world prices post 2003 and contributed to the expansion in exports, as higher international oil prices that did not translate into commensurately higher domestic prices encouraged the private companies to sell abroad.

A point to note is that in the period after 2011, India experienced severe exchange rate depreciation but its real exchange rate appreciated owing to domestic inflationary pressure. Taking a dummy for the quarters following 2011 Q4 reveals that the appreciation of the real exchange rate tended to reduce exports and imports, opening to question whether pronounced depreciation has the expected impact on trade.

This divergence observed in the response of oil and non-oil components of exports and imports makes a case for analysing trade at a higher level of disaggregation. The separate analysis of oil and non-oil trade shows that the nature of the commodity as well as the kinds of incentive extended to a sector can have an impact on the exchange rate-export relationship for that commodity. Therefore, in Chapters 3 and 4, exports and imports were broken down into major commodities and by major trading partners.

Commodity-wise analysis

Carrying on from the bifurcation of aggregates, the book proceeded to analyse the question in the context of further disaggregate trade, by top commodities. As is expected, the commodity-based disaggregation of exports shows that the impact observed across major commodities is not consistent, either. That is, exports of primary, mineral, and labour intensive and capital intensive manufactured commodities differ in their response to the exchange rate. Exchange rate movement is shown to matter in the case of labour intensive exports, such as gems and jewellery and apparel, whereas it seems to be ineffective in the case of primary or mineral-based exports. In the case of exports of manufactures, although the estimated coefficient is of the right sign, i.e. depreciation (appreciation) leads to higher (lower) exports, it is insignificant. To verify, the firm level information was analysed for manufacturing exports. The result here was corroborated – the coefficient was found to be significant.[2]

Even among the category of manufactures, there is a product specific response. For example, pharmaceuticals, machinery, gems and jewellery, and apparel are all commodities for which exchange rate depreciation (appreciation) leads to higher (lower) value of exports. All of these are commodities for which India faces stiff price competition. On the other hand, there are commodities such as vehicles, organic chemicals, cotton, and cereals for which no adjustment was observed in the value of exports in response to changes in the exchange rate.

These divergences can be explained to a large extent by policy interventions; for example, organic chemicals and vehicles, commodities as inputs by units located abroad. Therefore, even when India's exchange rate appreciates, the demand for such inputs may not decline. On the other hand, cotton and cereals have both witnessed favourable price movements. For example, in the case of cotton, better prices offered for exports led to the diversion of some of the cotton output to the export market at the cost of supply to domestic weavers. Export of cereals consisting largely of rice is subject to a stop-go policy whereby the government bans exports in periods of rising global prices. In the recent period, a ban was imposed on export of rice. This ban lasted for about four years between 2007 and 2011. During this period, the FCI stocked rice which it later exported upon the lifting of the ban at a lower minimum export price in order to compete with other rice exporters. Thus, the lack of response to the exchange rate can be assigned to reasons such as differences in domestic and export prices, where a wedge between the two can switch incentives to supply in favour of the export market. The lack of response of exports of mineral fuels can also be related to such price differences that make it more profitable for domestic producers to sell abroad.

Similar to the exports, imports too were analysed based on categorisation of commodities into manufactures, export related imports and primary imports. It has been shown in this book that the expansion in India's production as well as exports has been accompanied by a rise in import intensity. Therefore, import of manufactures is inelastic, meaning that depreciation (appreciation) leads to higher (lower) value of imports. Such result is in fact observed, for some commodities such as machinery, fertilisers, organic chemicals, and iron and steel were found to expand (decline) with the exchange rate depreciation (appreciation). For others, the exchange rate had no impact on imports. For oil imports, be they overall or bilateral, the exchange rate did not have a significant impact.

Now, these aggregates must be tied in with the statistical evidence for the disaggregate. Although the aggregate analysis suggests that oil imports expanded with depreciation, the disaggregate suggests otherwise. It is possible to reconcile such divergence, since the impact for the aggregates is quarterly, and in the long run this may not be true (long-run coefficient reported in Chapter 2).

Similarly, in Chapter 2, for non-oil imports it was seen that exchange rate depreciation (appreciation) leads to a decrease (increase) in imports. However, the results for disaggregated trade revealed that while imports of some commodities expand (decline) with depreciation (appreciation), there are others for which no response was observed. Some commodities for which the coefficient for exchange rate was insignificant, the direction of impact was as expected. Therefore, while there is divergence in the estimated response of import by commodities, in the aggregate the exchange rate has expected impact. Therefore, the results for the aggregate as well as disaggregate trade can be reconciled.

Country-wise analysis

The country-wise analysis is the final set of evidence that strengthen the conclusion of earlier chapters that the impact depends on product composition and concentration. Countries such as the USA, the UK, Belgium, Hong Kong, and UAE for which commodities such as gems and jewellery, apparel, machinery, and pharmaceuticals form a large part of exports are also countries for which exchange rate was found to be significant. In the case of imports as well, the predominance of items such as fertilisers, machinery, organic chemicals and machinery led to inelasticity.

It was seen that for the UK and Belgium, where labour intensive goods such as apparel and gems and jewellery form a large part of exports, the exchange rate was found to have a significant impact on exports; whereas for Germany and the Netherlands, the exchange rate was shown to have no impact. Though the EU provides a large market for India's labour intensive exports, manufactures such as machinery, vehicles (or parts thereof) and organic chemicals accounted for a larger share in 2014 than in the late 1990s. The importance of products such as vehicles and chemicals in exports was observed for the Netherlands and Germany. The difference in the product composition explains the difference in the estimated coefficients for exports within the region.

The other two countries where the exchange rate was shown to have no impact on exports are Japan and Singapore. In case of exports to both these countries, there has been an increase in exports of petroleum products, which contributes approximately 40 per cent and 54 per cent to exports of Japan and Singapore respectively. Excluding petroleum from exports to these countries revealed that while for Singapore the exchange rate had an impact on the non-oil component of exports, for Japan no such change was observed. The decline in export of apparel and gems and jewellery to Japan along with the increased predominance of primary exports can be used to explain the difference between the two countries in terms of the response of exports to exchange rate changes.

Similarly, for Saudi Arabia, the major items of exports include rice, meat, and chemicals. Exports of all of these products were shown to have no relationship with the exchange rate. Therefore, for exports to Saudi Arabia, the exchange rate was found to have no impact.

Hong Kong, the USA, and UAE are all among the top export destinations for India, with exports of commodities such as apparel, gems and jewellery, and petroleum products. While exports of petroleum products to these countries have increased, labour intensive commodities still contribute a significant proportion. As is expected, exchange rate depreciation (appreciation) leads to higher (lower) exports with these countries.

China has emerged as a significant trading partner for India. It is a major destination for India's exports, as well as a source of imports. The results for China do not conform with the general results reported in this book; it is an exception to the rule of commodity composition. For China, even though exports consist of items for which the exchange rate was found to be insignificant, the estimated coefficient for China showed that exports increase with depreciation. Exports to China, as was shown in Chapter 4, comprise mainly mineral based exports (petroleum products, copper, and iron ore) and raw materials such as cotton and textile yarn. In the analysis of commodity-wise exports, it was seen that for exports of petroleum and cotton, the exchange rate had no significant impact. However, the result that China's exports respond with an increase (decline) to exchange rate depreciation (appreciation) cannot be attributed to commodity composition. One possible explanation of this result is that while for these commodities the exchange rate does not matter in general, in the case of China prices determined by exchange rate do matter. China tends to source its imports of ores and cotton (the main products imported from India) from countries that provide these commodities at a lower price. For example, China imports iron ore from countries such as Australia and Brazil that are known to supply iron ore at the lowest price. Further, it imports copper from Latin American countries such as Chile and Peru. Similarly, cotton exports from India compete with those from the USA. Thus, the cheaper sources of imports for such commodities make exports to China sensitive to the exchange rate.

Imports from most trading partners do not respond to changes in the exchange rate. However, it is observed that where imports are heavily concentrated in a single product, such as Hong Kong, the UK, Switzerland, and Belgium, exchange rate depreciation (appreciation) results in an increase (decrease) in value of imports. India imports precious stones from Belgium and Hong Kong, whereas it imports gold from Switzerland; as for the UK, India imports silver. For these countries, imports increase (decrease) in value whenever the exchange rate depreciates (appreciates). China has emerged as a major source of imports for commodities such as machinery, organic chemicals, and fertilisers. The growing reliance on China has, therefore, manifested in inelasticity of imports.

Therefore, in the case of bilateral trade, the product composition is a major determinant of the estimated impact of exchange rate.

Policy conclusion

Recent depreciation of the rupee has brought to fore the discussion on trade-exchange rate linkages. There has been support as well as dismissal of the strong relationship between the two. In this context, it is important to ask if the exchange rate is available as a policy tool to influence exports as well as imports by India. The World Economic Outlook of 2015 posited this question for several economies including India. The IMF concluded that "policy views based on the traditional relationship between exchange rates and trade are still tenable." Similarly, there are those who propose the use of exchange rate depreciation as a tool to boost exports. For example, Nayyar (2016)[3] suggests that

> the time has come to let the rupee depreciate not just in nominal terms but also in real terms. A more appropriate exchange rate would help reduce the balance of trade deficit to manageable proportions by stimulating exports and dampening imports.

On the contrary, former RBI governor Raghuram Rajan[4] upheld the view that devaluation was not the appropriate tool to encourage exports. Situated in the recent debate on the matter, the results shed light on the appropriateness of the exchange rate as a tool to influence trade. There seems to be renewed optimism that the exports may be lifted in times of such depreciation as would expansion of imports be deterred. This conclusion warrants a thorough examination, which had thus far been few, if any. Taking on the subject, the book examined the question for overall, commodity specific trade as well as bilateral trade. Enough has been spoken about rather consistent evidence about commodity driven impact. This brings us to the crux of the matter: if the observed causalities hold, then what must policy makers do? Observe the aggregates and let the exchange rate be, or track the sectors and step in to correct an adverse effect? To begin with, the policy maker looking to influence trade must of course possess a nuanced understanding of the structure and should consider equal trade policy and monetary management.

Having said that, the prospect of encouraging exports by letting the exchange rate depreciate is limited to the extent of labour intensive commodities as well as some manufactures such as machinery and pharmaceuticals. To the extent that exports serve as inputs to production in other countries, the exchange rate cannot serve as a tool to promote exports of those commodities. Alternatively, an exchange rate appreciation adversely impacts exports of some of the major commodities mentioned earlier. Therefore, though the depreciation can augment such exports and possibly inhibit imports, an appreciation will surely adversely impact exports of some major commodities such as gems and jewellery, machinery, pharmaceuticals, and apparel that contribute a significant share to India's exports. Therefore, it may be in the interest of such industries to encourage that policy makers intervene to stall significant appreciation of the rupee.

However, the policies adopted by the government to boost exports must be rationalised. The growth in exports in the last decade was accompanied by a substantial expansion in the exports of petroleum products, which resulted from the perverse domestic incentives. Any policy that seeks to achieve growth of exports by incentivising such commodities can be detrimental for the overall trade position, since the exports are shown to be import-dependent. Given that Make in India is emblematic of govern-ment's aim to boost export of manufactures, the import dependency poses a dilemma from the standpoint of overall trade deficit. Thus, any export promotion scheme should bolster domestic capacity to service production of export goods than to allow relatively easy access to imported inputs as has been done in the past.[5]

As for imports, the overall imports do respond to the exchange rate, i.e. an exchange rate appreciation leads to higher imports. While this holds at the aggregate level, in the analysis for the disaggregated trade, it is seen that for some commodities as well as for some countries, imports expand with depreciation. The exchange rate serves as a useful tool to influence imports in the aggregate. However, to manage imports in commodities such as precious stones and metals, tariffs have proven to be a more useful policy instrument.[6]

The detailed work in this book sought to find evidence on whether exchange rate changes have any bearing on merchandise trade of India. No consistent evidence exists so far, and to substantiate, this book presented expansive analysis. All preceding discussions lead us to the answer that trade, also suggested in theory, depends not just on exchange rates but on demand and policy interventions. Yet, if those managing fluctuations in cur-rency are to make a decision of whether to intervene in the market, they must counter appreciation better, since a depreciation will positively affect major export items while reducing imports.

Notes

1 Similarity is measured using an index constructed by UNCTAD by taking three-digit SITC classification. The value of the index declined from approximately 0.5 in 1995 to 0.4 in 2013.
2 The firm level analysis gives a significant coefficient that suggests an expansion in exports when exchange rate depreciates. The difference between the analysis bases on overall and firm level data could be assigned to the differences in sample where the firm level information may be comprised more of products that are sensitive to exchange rate changes.
3 "Great fall of India's exports," January 2016
4 "Rupee devaluation not the right tool to boost exports: Raghuram Rajan," March 2016.
5 Duty drawback schemes encourage imports for production.
6 Imports of gold that constitute a large part of imports within gems and jewellery are known to respond to customs tariff. The rise in the current account deficit prompted the government to raise the tariff on gold from 2 per cent to 10 per cent through four revisions between January 2012 and August 2013. The increase in tariff arrested the growth in gold imports and led to a decline in the current account deficit. On the other hand, the expansion of imports is not just driven by the growth in domestic demand, but also by the government's measures to boost refining capacity. Therefore, for imports, incentives offered or disincentives intro-duced by the government play a greater role than the exchange rate.

References

Aizenman, J., Binici, M. and Hutchison, M.M., 2014. *The transmission of Federal Reserve tapering news to emerging financial markets* (No. w19980). National Bureau of Economic Research.

"Corporate tax avoidance by multinational firms," 2013, available at www.europarl. europa.eu/RegData/bibliotheque/briefing/2013/130574/LDM_BRI(2013)130574_REV1_EN.pdf

Francis, S., 2015. *India's manufacturing sector export performance: A focus on missing domestic inter-sectoral linkages.* New Delhi: Institute for Studies in Industrial Development, available at http://www.isid.org.in/pdf/WP182.pdf.

Postscript

The world we are in now

The empirical analysis in this book stops at year 2014. Not only has the economic growth in India been jarred by a series of *reforms* such as GST and the Insolvency and Bankruptcy code, but the globe too has witnessed some upheaval. Just as global demand began to recover in 2017 major economies, starting with the United States, began signalling the adoption of inward looking policies. The United States, for example, employed tariffs and sanctions on trade of specific commodities exported by China as well as India. The main point of contention for trade with India was the offer of export subsidy, such as that to export oriented units. To add to the unsettling developments, the UK initiated the process of moving out of the European Union. As a result, India's exports, which have been shown to depend on global demand, now confront unstable markets. In the light of such developments the reader may be curious if the causation or impact as shown in this book still holds. As was shown in this book, the adjustment follows a process, and tracing some of the related trends allows us to comment on whether we still observe the results estimated for the period until 2014.

After the short period of divergence where the real effective exchange rate appreciated in spite of nominal exchange rate depreciation, there was a reversal. It is seen in Figure P.1. The movements in REER have been in tandem with those in NEER. Therefore, even recent data corroborate weak pass through, if at all from exchange rate to domestic prices.

Structurally, India's trade has more or less remained the same. The major commodities traded by India as well as trading partners were listed in the earlier chapters of this book (3 and 4). The only important change that is observed during this period is that the share of oil exports has declined from a fifth to close to 12 per cent.

Over the period April 2012 to October 2018, the real exchange rate after a very sharp depreciation in August 2013 appreciated continuously through December 2017. During this period, the exports picked up and the trade deficit declined in October 2013, February 2014, and 2016. Note that except for the first, on none of the occasions did the exchange rate depreciate, suggesting that the relationship between exports remains weak.

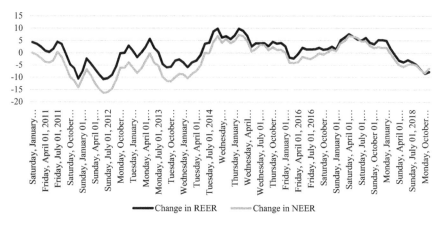

Figure P.1 Percentage change in REER and NEER, January 2011 to October 2018

Source: Computed from RBI

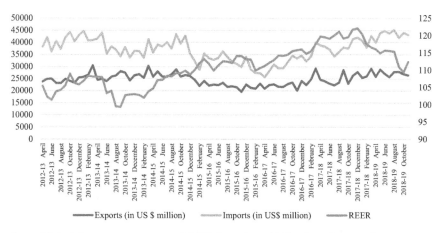

Figure P.2 India's export, imports, and REER from April 2012–13 to October 2018–19

Source: Constructed from RBI

Only in the instance of the sharp depreciation following December 2017 did exports pick up, but only slightly, and they later stabilised. It is possible to ask, why despite such sharp depreciation and decline in oil exports have the exports not grown dramatically? In all of the estimates, it was shown that the demand side factors play an important role. That is, world demand for exports drive India's exports. The recent global developments could have potentially dampened the growth. On the other hand, after the decline in imports until April 2016, there was a reversal where imports have shown a continued upward trend and, even with the recent depreciation imports expanded, only stabilising in the last two months (Figure P.2).

These trends substantiate that even in tumultuous times, the relationships that were estimated in the book survive. Consequently, the policy conclusions derived herein remain intact. There is merit that the question be examined over time; however, it is hoped that the puzzle presented at the start has been pieced together to some extent and that the exchange rates may not drive overall trade.

Index